THE GRADE CRICKETER

TEA AND NO SYMPATHY

THE GRADE CRICKETER

TEA AND NO SYMPATHY

**DAVE EDWARDS, SAM PERRY
AND IAN HIGGINS**

ALLEN&UNWIN
SYDNEY·MELBOURNE·AUCKLAND·LONDON

First published in 2017

Allen & Unwin
83 Alexander Street
Crows Nest NSW 2065
Australia
Phone: (61 2) 8425 0100
Email: info@allenandunwin.com
Web: www.allenandunwin.com

Cataloguing-in-Publication details are available
from the National Library of Australia
www.trove.nla.gov.au

ISBN 978 1 76063 131 4

Set in 13/17 pt Adobe Caslon by Midland Typesetters, Australia
Printed and bound in Australia by Griffin Press

10 9 8 7 6 5 4 3 2

CONTENTS

1

THE OFFER

Here I was, on a crisp April morning, standing on the side of the road outside my house, waiting for a bald maniac to pick me up. Nuggsy had already exceeded the maximum demerit points allowable for a car licence, having copped three separate speeding fines and a DUI over Christmas, but we could never break with tradition. After all, Nuggsy and I had been carpooling to cricket games for as long as I could remember. His yellowing 1994 Nissan Pulsar had clocked up 307,806 kilometres and taken us to hundreds of cricket grounds all across the state. It was precisely the kind of vehicle that would have belonged to a serial killer (if said serial killer had a *Triple M Rocks the Footy* bumper sticker and a garbage bag for a side window). Nonetheless, it was a pleasant sight to see him hooning around the bend on this Saturday morning, even if he was doing roughly eighty-five k's in a forty zone.

Nuggsy's front wheel crudely scraped the kerb as he pulled to a stop. If he had a hub cap it would have probably incurred considerable damage. He yanked the handbrake with typical aggression, wound down the window and shouted, voice straining over the top of Screaming Jets' 1991 hit 'Better'.

'Hop in, big fella!'

I heaved my kit into the boot and made my way around to the passenger door. As always, I was greeted by six or seven empty Mother energy drinks on the tattered front seat, each containing perhaps ten or twenty millilitres of backwash. The car stunk like sweaty cricket kit, guarana, and Lynx Africa. Not for the first time, I wondered why cricketers always chose Africa as their preferred deodorant when there were so many other fragrances available in the Lynx product line. With a single arm movement, I swiped the 500-millilitre cans onto the floor and hopped in.

'We doing drive-through?'

'Nah, we've got a bit of time, big dog. Let's eat in.'

I couldn't quite put my finger on it but Nuggsy seemed different today. For starters, he wasn't poisonously hung-over. It wasn't unheard of for Nuggsy to head straight to a game from a night out. Once he actually wore his whites out on a Friday night in order to conserve time the next morning. That night he'd managed to convince a woman he was a state cricketer—not for the first time, may I add. One thing led to another and he ended up getting, in his words, a 'thumping blowjob' in the back of his car outside our home ground. He rolled up to the ground with a red wine stain on his cricket vest, still feasting on that perfect still-drunk-yet-not-hungover ratio that inspires irrational confidence in even the most introverted types. We all roared with approval as he provided us with an animated instructional guide to 'smashing a bird' in a hatchback vehicle. He took 6-18 that day and bowled us to a historic victory. The woman in question, as was so often the case with these types of stories, was never heard of again.

But today, Nuggsy was stone sober and conspicuously quiet. I chalked this down to nerves, for it had been years since we'd played in a grand final. As we weaved our way through the busy McDonald's car park, Nuggsy craned his neck around, eyes darting, as if plagued by a sudden acute bout of paranoia.

'You alright, mate?' I enquired, letting out a bemused snort.

'Nah, just tough to find a park here, hey,' Nuggsy replied, arching his back to look behind him as he edged forward in search of a spot.

It was a Saturday morning, after all, and McDonald's was already teeming with young families. Dozens of sprightly young kids in basketball singlets and cricket uniforms skipped in and out of the restaurant, clutching Happy Meals and thickshakes, flanked by dutiful parents. Meanwhile, two blokes in their early thirties clad in training kit were stinging for a pre-match Bacon & Egg McMuffin.

A pink Kia ducked out and Nuggsy, ever alert, swung his car forward into the vacant parking space. A disabled parking space.

'Result!' he roared, suddenly alive. 'I'm the fucking king at jagging a park!'

It was always about status with Nuggsy. Whether it was his cricket, his sex life, fantasy football or finding a park, Nuggsy had to attribute himself some sort of rank. I made a mental note to research the etymology of the term 'jagging'. What did it mean to 'jag' something? Only cricketers could invent meaningless verbiage and lend it primal aggression. In well over ten years, I'd never seen him do a reverse park. Always headfirst.

We hopped out of the car and made our way into McDonald's.

'It's on me, bud. The usual?'

'Umm, yeah. Thanks, mate.'

We'd eaten together on hundreds of occasions, many times in this exact eatery, but not once had he reached for the tab. Nuggsy collected our meals and took the tray over in search of a seat.

'Yep, over in the corner, there's a spot.'

A white-haired gentleman was seated alone in a booth with his back to us, reading a tabloid newspaper. As Nuggsy approached, he placed a gentle hand on the man's shoulder, a move that appeared strangely personal. The man rotated his torso around with discernible difficulty and smiled.

'Alan, wonderful to see you as always,' a familiar baritone voice said.

Geoffrey Beveridge, a stocky man in his mid to late sixties, was the president of my former grade cricket club. I knew Nuggsy had kept in touch with Bevo over the years, but it was nonetheless a surprise to see him here at McDonald's, all alone, on the morning of our grand final. Bevo had held the position of club president for the past forty years, the longest stint in the history of the competition. This forty-year run was inclusive of his two-year home detention stretch for tax fraud in the early nineties, which served to enhance his reputation if anything. No one really knew if he'd ever played the game, although like all senior club officials, he did little to quash rumours that he played a bit of state cricket in the 1960s.

Bevo was probably most famous for his habit of putting a five grand bar tab on at the clubhouse whenever all five grades got up. This was, and remains, the only time that blokes in first and second grade ever took an interest in what was going on in the lower grades. Bevo would walk around with his Bluetooth earpiece in and provide live updates on play at Hislop Oval #2, scrawling them on the clubhouse whiteboard. This was the pre–social media era, of course. Now most grade cricket clubs provide rolling updates for their Twitter followers throughout the course of a day. There really is a lot of useless shit on the internet.

Aside from that, Bevo also had a well-documented proclivity for young Asian women. Every season we looked forward to Bevo debuting a new, scantily clad 'female friend' at round one selection night. These relationships were all presumably forged via the internet since he only frequented two establishments, our home ground clubhouse and the bar directly opposite the clubhouse, Frankie's (although he did spend an alarming amount of time in Southeast Asia).

In short, Bevo was your archetypal club president: morally bankrupt, inexplicably wealthy and perennially involved in divorce proceedings of some sort.

'G'day, Bevo,' I replied.

It had been years since we'd crossed paths. His beady eyes were barely visible under his hooded eyelids; his skin exceptionally taut for a man of his age. It glistened in the harsh McDonald's lighting, giving the impression he'd recently been caught in an unfortunate house fire.

'Well, well. Ready for the big game?' he asked, placing the form guide down on the table.

'Yep, sure am.'

Today was a big day for Bevo. His club had three grades playing off in grand finals. In recent years they had experienced an unprecedented wave of success both on and off the field, a resurgence that just so happened to coincide with the moment that Nuggsy and I left the club. They'd gotten rid of a lot of the older blokes like Damo, Bruiser and Bretty and brought in a new wave of youngsters—and with it a professional culture that was helping to attract new, lucrative sponsorship opportunities and improved facilities. Truth be told, the club was barely recognisable from the days when Nuggsy and I used to play there, except for the fact that Bevo was still at the helm, putting five thousand dollars on the bar when all five grades got up, a now increasingly regular occurrence.

Bevo turned to face Nuggsy, who had assumed the spot next to him.

'So, Alan. Are we all onboard with how today is going to pan out?'

Nuggsy hesitated for a moment before looking at me. He lowered his gaze sheepishly.

'Haven't told him yet.'

'What's going on?' I enquired, a shade too much urgency in my voice.

Bevo smiled insouciantly and leaned back into the booth. He prodded Nuggsy gently with his elbow, an invitation to divulge more information.

Nuggsy placed his Bacon & Egg McMuffin down on the tray and looked around carefully before leaning forward on the table to address me directly.

'Mate, there's a fix on,' he whispered solemnly.

What?

'We're throwing this game.'

I sat there, completely stunned. I wasn't quite sure whether he was joking, but his ashen face was cause for concern. Nuggsy hadn't looked this pale since he caught the zika virus on our post-season trip to Miami.

'Let me elaborate here, Alan, if I may,' Bevo intervened genially. 'I have placed a personal bet on the outcome of your match. Should your team lose today, I stand to win fifty thousand dollars. I have offered Alan ten thousand to ensure that happens.'

Match-fixing. Well, this was a new one.

I knew that grade cricket was dark and depressing but up to this point I had been oblivious to its sinister underbelly. I wondered whether I'd been unwittingly involved in any other fixed matches over the years. After all, I'd played the majority of my career alongside Nuggsy. Had he been fixing matches for a decade? The 30 I scored in second grade back in 2007? The 2-27 against the second-bottom team? Even my maiden grade cricket century, which seemed to come all too easily in retrospect? All these wonderful personal achievements were now cast under serious doubt. I shuddered involuntarily. Was my entire *life* a lie?

'Sorry, guys. I . . . I can't be involved in this,' I managed.

With gangster-like poise, Bevo allowed my sentence to hang in the air for a moment before twisting his mouth into a wry grin.

'Alan, my boy, perhaps you two can go off and have a quiet word?'

Nuggsy rose from his seat and gesticulated for me to follow. We made our way into the McDonald's play equipment area. Despite the tense scenario, I couldn't help but note the absurdity of the setting. Two grade cricketers standing in the play area of a fast-food franchise, surrounded by young children pepped up on refined sugars, discussing match-fixing in a third grade final.

'Mate,' I started, as always. (Even when addressing their mortal enemy Australian men will employ this term of endearment.) 'What the fuck are you up to here?'

Nuggsy was nervously fidgeting with the sleeve of his training shirt, hopping from foot to foot. I noticed a bead of sweat snaking its way down his forehead.

'Mate, can you just help a brother out? I've never asked much of you,' he implored, clearly forgetting that he had asked me for a six-hundred-dollar loan less than forty-eight hours ago.

'Seriously, Nuggsy,' I responded, adopting a fatherly tone, 'how did you get involved in this?'

With a hanging head, Nuggsy confessed that he had been taking out cash loans from one of those unscrupulous companies that claim to offer money 'within the hour'. The TV advertisements are charmingly quirky, designed to divert your attention from the exorbitant interest rates, not to mention the substantial fees for late payments. Nuggsy was the perfect target market for this type of company, as most grade cricketers are: male, thirties, cash-poor, prone to vice. In truth, the exact same market that sports-betting agencies tend to focus their advertising on. But after doing this for a year or so, Nuggsy was now, by his own admission, 'balls deep in debt' and required a serious cash injection in order to get out of this sticky situation. Nuggsy had gone to his parents for money but they'd turned him away. Now living over in France after long, successful careers of their own, it seemed they finally resented the continual dig into their retirement fund to support their idiot adult son. With nowhere to go, Nuggsy had approached Bevo in the hope of a handout, but the devious Bevo had sniffed an opportunity—and now, as it turned out, Nuggsy was in deep. Real deep.

'And why is Bevo doing this?'

Nuggsy laughed. 'Mate, Bevo's been fixing matches for years. All these bastards have.'

'But who's he betting against?'

'He's betting against Davo.'

Rodger Davies was *our* club president! Two club presidents betting on the outcome of a grade cricket final. Un-fucking-believable. But . . . was it, really? Actually, it all kind of made sense suddenly. From the outside, club presidents poured thousands of dollars into grade cricket with seemingly no expectation of return, aside from the meaningless power one wields from being the president of a cricket club. But perhaps there *was* a return, after all? Perhaps grade cricket was completely *rigged*—nothing more than a plaything for rich white men to fuck with, placing bets and fixing matches unbeknown to the players themselves, save for a few key conduits like Nuggsy, who were able to bridge these murky waters.

The rest of us were mere pawns.

Nuggsy was a fucking basket case, no doubt. But he was, nonetheless, my best friend. Ever since my best non-cricket friend, Finn, had moved to Berlin to 'make it' as a musician (i.e. play DJ sets at 4 a.m. in sparsely populated nightclubs where all the patrons are fucked up on ketamine), Nuggsy and I had become inseparable. It was Nuggsy who befriended me at one of my first training sessions all those years ago, when I was just a young kid trying to make my way in grade cricket and no one else would even acknowledge my existence. A few years my senior, he'd taken me under his wing and taught me everything I needed to know: namely, that I needed to drastically improve my rig if I was ever going to move up the grades. We worked out at the same gym for years, just two blokes desperately striving for the perfect V-shaped torso, but it was more than that. We shared a dream of playing cricket at the highest possible level.

I thought back to this time last year, when Lara and I were on holiday in Japan. We were completely enamoured by the beautiful *sakura* gardens, the cherry blossoms that bloom from March to April and signify the arrival of spring. But while there I was also fascinated to learn about a centuries-old tradition that still holds firm in Japanese society today, a unique seniority-based relationship between *senpai* (先輩) and *kōhai* (後輩). It bore some similarity to a mentor/protégé relationship in Western culture where an older person imparts his wisdom and experience to a chosen youngster. In Japan these types of senior/junior relationships are most prevalent in the schoolyard and the workplace, but they are also found across all of Japanese society, including amateur sporting teams.

However, like many age-based systems, this relationship can easily become subject to abuse of power. It's not unknown for a Japanese *senpai* to take advantage of his *kōhai*, ordering him to undertake demeaning tasks—or even break the law—at their behest. The younger person, who feels indebted to his elder, is compelled to obey. I later learned that bullying is deeply rooted in the *senpai/kōhai* culture, and that Japanese people prefer to suffer in silence than stand up for themselves. Until this very moment, here in the McDonald's play area, I hadn't made the link between Japanese cultural values and grade cricket, but right now the parallels seemed clear. I wondered whether this type of thing was happening at an amateur Japanese baseball club as we spoke. Having established my trust and friendship over a decade, Nuggsy was deviously leveraging his *senpai* status for personal and financial gain. Even though I was now a veteran of grade cricket with ten or so years under my belt, Nuggsy's influence had yet to wane. In fact, his emotional hold over me was stronger than I'd ever realised. Could I turn my back on the person who had given me everything? The one bloke who had my back at all times? The man who had taught me everything I needed to know about how to survive in the tough, feudalistic society of grade cricket and made me who I was today?

Nuggsy stood in front of me, his long arms outstretched like a pauper's. Tears had gathered in his eyes, seemingly one blink away from careening down his cheeks. I'd never seen him so vulnerable, so emotionally naked.

'Please, big fella. I need this . . .'

Despite the situation, I couldn't help but be moved. Let's be clear: Nuggsy was a bloke who had no qualms coming off fourteen yards in fast-fading light at training, deriving pleasure from striking the unsuspecting batsman on the fleshy inner thigh. Once he famously refused to walk after being caught at cover in a third grade semi-final. I had been championing the value of vulnerability to him for some time—no doubt a product of Lara's influence—and even though he was proposing I participate in malevolent corruption, I was somehow strangely proud of him. Because while Nuggsy was clearly broken, he was now, at long last, being honest.

I took a breath, squared my body to his, focused my gaze on his watery eyes and placed a solitary hand on his impressive shoulder.

God, he had delts for days.

'Nuggsy,' I started, my stare unwavering, 'are you absolutely sure you want to do this?'

Nuggsy was a fast-talking raconteur with a bogan tinge, but he sensed the gravity of my question. He took a deep breath as I removed my palm from his shoulder, for it had now hung there too long. Nuggsy raised his own mammoth hands and fixed them forcefully on my shoulders.

'Mate, I don't *want* this,' he implored. 'I *need* this.'

He rocked me back and forth while uttering his final verbal gambit, causing me to readjust my balance as the Havaiana on my right foot slipped on the McDonald's asphalt. His eyes had now morphed into a bulging mass of white sclera, brown iris and tiny black pupils.

'Settle down, Nuggsy!' I said. 'Just settle down.'

He removed his paws from me. I slid my thong back on, gazed into the distance and thought about my connection to cricket, a relationship that had more or less defined my entire self-worth, and alarmingly so. Irritatingly so. Disastrously so. It's said blood runs thicker than water; in my view, friends were more important than grade cricket, or some shit. The game had given me little else but pain and social dysfunction, anyway. I was ready to answer.

'Alright, mate,' I said, taking his hand to shake it. 'What do you need me to do?'

'Gentlemen!' exclaimed Bevo, his face beaming as we headed back to his faux leather corner booth. He must have noticed Nuggsy's elated expression as he bounded over with the same enthusiastic ferocity of the children playing outside. I, meanwhile, sidled over with hands in pockets. The answer was clear, but Bevo sought confirmation anyway.

'Lads. Now, tell me: do we have good news?'

'The Nuggler has produced!' Nuggsy cried, slamming his enormous hand onto the plastic table between us.

Eyes downcast, I managed a meek thumbs up. But there was no time for high-fiving, fist-bumping or whatever weird shit people do to celebrate a basic agreement these days.

'So,' Nuggsy continued. 'Want me to tell old mate here how we're going to get this done?'

It appeared I was 'old mate', and I was about to be fed the gruesome details of this project.

'Go ahead, Nuggsy. This is your show, son,' Bevo replied, winking.

Obviously, this wasn't Nuggsy's 'show' at all. Bevo and his club president cadre had conjured this racket, and Nuggsy was just a necessary tool in its execution. There was something deeply sinister about Bevo wanting Nuggsy, a bloke who could barely manage his breakfast order fifteen minutes earlier, to feel in charge of this.

'Righto, just give us a sec while I run him through it. No interruptions.'

Nuggsy lowered his voice and leaned forward over the table to speak in a hushed tone.

'As you know, mate, we're going to lose the grand final today.'

He let the words sit for a little while. Admittedly, I did have to allow them to sink in. I thought about the consistent training at least three guys had done throughout the year, the efforts made to rally parents and friends to come along to the Big Day, the fact that many thought they sat on the cusp of their best sporting achievement to date. Nuggsy sensed this, gave me a second to compute it all, and moved on.

'It's a result-based bet—nothing exotic riding on it. Doesn't need to get done in a certain number of overs, and no one needs to bowl any no balls. We just need to influence the match to make sure the other mob gets up. They win. We lose. They win the premiership. We get nothing. They sing a song. We act dejected. Once that happens, we'll get *bulk sheets*, courtesy of old boy Bevo here!'

Nuggsy gesticulated at Bevo, who was still beaming back at me. I had a few questions.

'Nuggsy, is anyone else involved in this? I mean, there are only two of us. Isn't there usually at least three or four?'

Nuggsy looked at Bevo, who replied firmly that no, it would just be us.

'So, let me get this straight,' I carried on. 'There is fifty grand riding on us losing this grand final, and you think the two of us can pull that off alone?'

'I know, it's a pretty decent rap, isn't it, mate?' Nuggsy grinned, trying to lighten the tone.

But I had to keep going.

'As you know, mate, I've averaged 10.47 this year. And you've had about four knocks all season. Your back is cooked and you've barely taken a pole since returning. I've only just started bowling again. Benno's in good nick—what if he hits a ton? Even if we fail—which is our ultimate goal— what if it's not enough?'

I was convinced my fears were well founded. I would never normally admit it outwardly, but I had been a pillar of mediocrity for the majority of the year. Sure, I'd recorded the occasional 30 or 40 (usually in the second innings after the opposition had already won, with no other result possible), but I had rarely been a threat otherwise. Then again, perhaps I was being too harsh on myself. As we entered the finals, Nuggsy, from nowhere, suggested to our skipper, Wizz, that I bowl a couple of off spinners to 'offer a different angle'. Formerly a medium pacer, I had recently reinvented myself as a part-time off spinner after being hit for what Nuggsy and others described as the 'biggest six I've ever seen in my life' in the final match of the preceding season. I figured that off spin is literally the easiest skill one can perform in cricket—no different from turning a doorknob clockwise in terms of the effort exuded.

Wizz was initially incredulous, rightly pointing out that as a notional right-arm off spinner, my angle was as far from 'different' as was possible in cricket. Nuggsy had looked at me, raising his eyebrows in mock surprise, before firing back at the skipper that, in fact, I had experienced 'quite a bit' of success from coming right arm around the wicket between umpire and crease, noting that my 'side-on action' apparently 'amplified the shape' of my deliveries and 'produced the prodigious overspin necessary for the roads they serve up in the finals'. These were his precise words, as though spoken verbatim from some inane analysis he'd heard on TV. Never mind that I looked like a bowler from 1910: chest-on, round arm with revolutions akin to a flying saucer—Nuggsy was adamant I should bowl. After bullying Wizz into submission, he would later tell me he was 'just keen to see me have a trundle' after prolonged boredom at first slip. Looking back, he'd probably just bet on us losing the match.

But bowling had brought something out in me. I'd managed to subdue a few free-scoring batsmen and had taken three wickets in our first final, followed by four in the next. We had a half-hearted attempt at a second innings in that game, too, which yielded me two more top-order wickets. It all meant I arrived in the grand final as a greater threat with ball in hand than bat, even if I was reluctant to admit that to myself. I was like the classic case of the promising young leg spinner in reverse: despite hours upon hours of practice, these youths, doubtless inspired by footage of Shane Warne, take to suburban grounds only to be subjected to horrific, colossal hitting. In reality, they have more to offer the actual scorecard with the bat, however much they feel otherwise. There are only so many double bouncers and full tosses you can take, I guess.

Nuggsy could see what I was thinking.

'Mate, you're a gun with the ball. A true *dangerman*,' he cooed. 'I wouldn't rule you out with the bat either. I'd say you're due some runs, and you're not batting five for nothing. But if you can just manage to remove yourself, that would be greatly appreciated.'

What was this 'greatly appreciated' shit, an office email sign-off?

'How do you suggest I *remove myself*, mate?' I challenged him.

'Oh, I don't know, however you normally do it! There's plenty of ways.'

'What's that supposed to mean?' I shot back, my sensitivity growing at the suggestion there were innumerable ways I could feasibly get out.

'Chip to short cover. Nick off. Fall over your crease, LBW. Miss a straight one. Cut uppishly, get through one too early and get a leading edge, get into a mix-up and run yourself out. I've seen you get out all those ways, mate. Just your usuals. Look, don't be offended, mate. I really think you can help us out here and, don't forget, we'll get some serious sheets for this.'

I wished he'd stop saying the word *sheets*.

'Fuck, alright,' I replied, my frustration building. 'And what about with the ball?'

'Give it plenty of air, bud. Keep yourself at five or six an over. Don't go for so many that Wizz takes you off, but not so little that—God forbid—you actually build some bloody pressure!'

'And don't take a catch, whatever you do!' Bevo chimed in.

Nuggsy and Bevo chinked their chocolate thickshakes. Both conspirators were now significantly more relaxed, satisfied with my commitment to their cause. I hadn't yet reflected on why they chose *me* to participate, but was surer of my own motivation for participating. Nuggsy was a mate and I wanted to help him out—that part was actually true. But beyond that, I knew that cricket had caused me nothing but pain. Trying to perform beyond my own warped expectations—and the expectations of others—on a weekly basis had exhausted me to breaking point. Cricket and my connection to it had been nothing but an infinite maze of false hope and crippling disappointment. *Yes*, I was going to try something else. I was going to get back at cricket. Sure, Nuggsy and I might go on to steal ten thousand bucks from the game about to take place, but in my defence, cricket had effectively stolen my youth. I was simply squaring a debt that the game owed me. And while I'd never admitted this to anyone, let alone myself, if there was anything I knew how to do well, it was fail.

With the fix now sorted, Nuggsy and I returned to the car. I sat stony-faced as Nuggsy jolted his shitty Pulsar out of the Maccas car park. Having spotted a tiny gap in traffic, he darted in ahead of a large bus, causing the vehicle to screech in order to avoid a collision.

'Result!' he yelped.

Nuggsy, who minutes earlier had been tearfully pleading with me to support his match-fixing project, now painted a picture of classic grade cricket contentment: window down, one hand on the steering wheel, banging his head along to Rage Against the Machine's 'Killing in the Name' as he veered dangerously in and out of lanes. Pulling into the ground, we passed several teammates rolling their kits along the gravelly driveway. Nuggsy gestured with the accepted grade cricket signal of acknowledgement: a lone finger raised off the steering wheel accompanied by the subtlest head nod possible. Today, he was the ultimate insurgent in plain clothing. He pulled the handbrake, bringing the car to a standstill, and looked at me.

'Let's do this, mate,' he said in a furtive baritone, deadly serious.

'Fucken oath,' I replied, now fuming at everything cricket had done to me.

2

FAILING IS AN ART

'I've got 9.31, Nuggsy! That's a fine, mate! For both of you!'
Wizz roared.

Wizz stood facing us, dramatically peering down at his
watch, its face clasped between his skinny pincer fingers,
eyeing the rest of the dressing-room for support.

'What do you reckon, boys? Is that a case or what?'

It was a typically sad attempt at jocularity from Wizz,
a slender man with an oddly shaped rig and thick-rimmed
glasses. Nuggsy and I sidled over to our usual corner spots
in the dressing-room, impervious to this tired ritual. To
be fair, Wizz was just trying to establish a bit of energy
among the group on this most important of days. In this
case, we were one minute late and now subject to a novelty
fine imposed by the captain. But there was a broader point.
In grade cricket, there's nothing like the casual humiliation

of a few to bond the many. The problem for Wizz was that he was captain in name only. Sure, he attended selection meetings, but that was because he was over thirty and wore a suit to training. He also had a 2004 BMW that, while over a decade old, suggested he had managed his money at some point in his life. In truth, though, Nuggsy ran the team, and Keith 'Wizz' Watson knew it.

'Think your watch is a bit quick again, Wizza,' Nuggsy replied, already rummaging around in his bag for a spare spike. 'We've got 9.29.'

'Now, Nuggsy,' Wizz started, keen to keep this going. 'My watch is the grade-A official timekeeper of this side, and I get the final call. It's 9.31, and that means you're getting the case. Boom!'

Having finally located a spare spike, Nuggsy had now commenced the always frustrating task of affixing it to his boot. The level of fine motor skill required here was a source of grave irritation for the hulking quick, who preferred to deal in large, macro physical motions. However, Wizza's retort had caused him to stop what he was doing. He placed the boot down on the ground as the whole team drew to a silence, keenly aware that another alpha play-off between our official captain and spiritual captain was brewing.

'Boom?' Nuggsy asked. 'Did you just say *boom?*'

Wizz sensed Nuggsy's incredulity. He knew he was no match for the bald, imposing Nuggsy, but he couldn't lose face. He opted for something in the middle.

'Geez, Nuggsy. You were late. Being late is a fine. It's the same for everyone. I'm trying to have a bit of a laugh.

Somebody's got to buy beers. Why do we have to do this every time? Can't you just go with it and cop the fine?'

Nuggsy sat silently, staring at Wizza. Then he reached into his kit and grabbed his bat. I was about to stand up to restrain him until I saw him grab his gloves too.

'C'mon, boys!' he said enthusiastically, springing to his feet. 'Let's get out there. What's the deck doing? Much in it?'

He made his way to the dressing-room door, where light spilled in from what was already a stunning day. Eight blokes followed him, though Wizz and I remained rooted to our positions, clearly bemused at what had just happened. I could hear Nuggsy saying far too audibly, 'Incredible bird last night, a Group One.' Cackling laughter broke out, as children in men's bodies made their way onto the dewy, sun-kissed oval. In so many ways, this was normal: we had arrived late, argued a fine, alpha'd the captain and commenced the telling of fictional sex stories.

The only difference—for me at least—was that I was about to throw the match.

Wizz won the toss and elected to bat. Nuggsy looked pensive after the result: we were batting first on a good wicket, which would undoubtedly make our job of losing harder. I was listed to bat at five, with Nuggsy at nine. The best we could do was fail—to be guaranteed, cheap wickets in both the middle and end of the innings. In many ways, it was nothing new. We sat down in the dressing-room, the team arranged in a perfect square around the perimeter of the concrete toilet block. Amid the mess of training gear, towels, the sound of velcro pad straps, and an alarming waft from the cubicles, Wizz arose with disproportionate grandiosity to speak. I snuck another glance at Nuggsy, now two-thirds of the way through an eye roll.

'Now. Boys. For many of you, this is the biggest game of your life. Heck, it's the biggest game of mine! But seriously, I have a couple of things I want to say before we bat. My main piece of advice is this: *think about it.* I want you to really, really think about it. I want us to be aggressive out there, but don't do anything silly. Let's take it to them, but let's be smart about it too. Run hard. Sharp singles. But no run-outs. Play your natural game, but let's remember: this is a *grand final.* It's different. This isn't a normal game. It will be tough. We will have to be patient. But let's be aggressive in our patience. Let's keep moving the game forward, and ticking the score over—and let's dig in too. Watch out for their opening quick—he's very accurate. So let's try to knock him off his length. But if he's hitting his length, let's defend. Rotate the strike too . . .'

Wizz's pre-game speech was nothing more than a litany of contradictions. For a man who worked in corporate communications—a profession where clear, unambiguous messaging is presumably vital—he had an uncanny ability to obfuscate the game of cricket. It was at this point that Nuggsy intervened, much to everyone's relief.

'I think we've had enough of the cricketing cliché salad, bud,' he barked, getting to his feet and assuming centre stage, hands on hips. 'Look, lads, it's a fucken great deck. I reckon we go really fucken hard at them. From one to eleven. Quick runs, then roll them. We've all played a few T20s—let's get at them! I know you can't win a one dayer

23

outright, but let's walk back into this dressing-room at the end of the day knowing we could have. We're better than these pricks. Seriously—Nev, Carts, pogo 'em from ball one. Forget your plans, don't give them a look, today's the day we make a statement. The earlier we get this done the earlier we get a beer ... Fuck it, I'll cop the fine and buy them myself if we're done by four!'

'*Wooooooooooooooo!*'

With just a few well-chosen words, Nuggsy had instantly whipped the entire team into a state of hysteria. It was a frenzy of team pride: guttural roars interspersed with thunderous backslaps and clapping that echoed around the concrete walls, sending an ominous warning to the opposition in the room next to us. It all belied the fact that we'd qualified sixth for this finals series and were playing a team undefeated in all three formats. Their line-up boasted four former first graders who were playing down the grades due to family commitments. This year their local paper had dubbed them 'The Third Grade Invincibles', such was their dominance, with 'a record to rival Bradman's team in 1948'. Nuggsy shot me a wink as we retired to the viewing area in front of the toilet block.

The innings didn't start well—although I guess it did, depending on who you asked. Nuggsy's pre-match pep talk had fired Nev up to the extent that he charged the very first ball of the day, toeing it to mid-off, triggering screams of joy from the opposition. The very next over, Carts was given LBW after being hit in the box attempting to slog sweep their opening quick. Slug, our number four, got in a mix-up after attempting a quick single to a ball that rolled straight back to the bowler. These were diabolical scenes.

All of a sudden, we were 3-5, and I was in.

I gathered my particulars, doing my best to block out the jubilant 'yiewing' from the opposition. For the first time in my cricket career, I barely felt a pang of nerves as I prepared to walk out to bat, for I already knew what would happen. This foresight didn't prevent me from nervously fumbling my helmet before affixing it to my head—some things never change—but I managed to catch it before it cannoned into the pavement beneath, a small victory. With the team in dire trouble, the pavilion was understandably silent.

'Do a job for us, mate. Stick with the plan. Backing you,' said Nuggsy.

He glared sternly at me as I passed him on my way to the centre. With the score at 3-5, he and I were already well on the way to money, beers and a middle finger to grade cricket. Meanwhile, I was curious about how quickly I could get myself out. It hadn't been a problem previously, but now I was more confident about succeeding in an innings than ever before. Without the burden of expectation and success, I felt perversely free.

'Here he is, boys!' cried some faceless kid standing at point.

He had all the accessories usually sported by overly enthusiastic young cricketers: speed dealer sunglasses; a perfectly bent brim on his cap; those ridiculous elbow guards for diving; chewing gum; sweat bands on both wrists; shirt buttoned, collar up. He prowled the point region with the maturity of an experienced policeman but couldn't have been older than eighteen.

'Another fucking cowboy!'

It was pointless exacerbating the inevitable by engaging in verbal battle. I asked the umpire, Simon, for 'two legs' and scratched away at my crease, scanning the field—not for gaps this time but for potential catchers.

One of their former first graders, Gerry Parmenter, had the rock in hand. Now in his early forties, Parmenter was still clearly a cut above the rest of us. He had a beautiful smooth run-up that allowed him to glide into the crease with effortless ease. It was widely known among grade cricketers that Parmenter had played a few seasons of county cricket with Warwickshire on a British passport (secured through a maternal connection) where he'd circuited with Brian Lara and a range of other colourful identities. At county level, his metronomic seamers had done enough to nick off the likes of Rahul Dravid and Younis Khan. Given his pedigree, I knew Parmenter would challenge the stumps and wobble the ball, so I planned on trying to scoop one to the off side somewhere, anywhere, and consign my team to an impossible scenario.

As expected, Parmenter's first delivery was right on the money, threatening the stumps and just full enough to ask me a question. That question was, specifically: 'Do you want to drive me? I am here, I am arcing ever-so-gently, and let's be honest, on this wicket I'm not going to do much when I eventually bounce off the surface. So, what do you want to do?' My goal was to get out, so my answer was clear: I would swing lustily, while leaning back fractionally in order to elevate the ball over cover. To my horror, the ball rocketed off my bat and slammed violently into the fence on the first bounce. It was the most audacious shot of my career—an inside-out drive over cover—and now I stood here, 4 not out, eyeballing a bloke that had taken over 250 first grade wickets. Parmenter gazed straight at me, arms crossed, befuddled. It was an outrageous decision to even attempt that shot on my first delivery, with the team at 3-5, let alone execute it to perfection.

'Wow,' said the faceless, over-enthusiastic kid at point sarcastically. 'Is this bloke kidding?'

His teammates said little. Like Parmenter, they had been rendered paralysed by the sequence of events.

Parmenter strode in now with a little more vigour than before. This delivery was a bouncer, heading straight at my face. Having already committed to playing the same shot, I found myself in no position to realistically repeat the inside-out drive over cover. Even worse, I had spent my entire cricket career so embarrassingly scared of the short ball (for a grown man) that I had not even considered moving towards a ball aimed at my head. Yet here I was, attempting to fix a match and thus arranging myself into utterly foreign positions, both mentally and physically. On the front foot to a short ball delivered by a former first grade opening bowler, my mind went blank. With no ability to duck, my eyes widened, I stood tall and delivered a crushing front-foot pull over forward square leg for six. My feet gracefully swivelled upon striking the ball, and later accounts described it as 'still rising' as it slammed into a tree by the boundary.

'Fuck *me!*' said Parmenter, who stood looking at me, hands on hips.

'Fuck *meeeee!*' Wizz chorused at the other end. 'Dougie Walters, eat your heart out!'

There was already a lot of silly shit happening. I was now 10 off two balls, having tripled our team total from 3-5 to 3-15. I had hit a professional cricketer over cover for four, and then front-foot pulled him for six, all while trying to get out.

Fuck, this tactic isn't working.

Parmenter's comeback delivery was on a good length, shaping towards the cordon. I strode out purposefully, struck it directly to short cover and took off for a quick (read suicidal) single. I could all but taste the cyanide in my mouth as I galloped towards the non-striker's end. The eighteen-year-old Michael Clarke wannabe at point moved quickly to the ball, but I was safely in my ground by the time he picked it up. What's more, I had unintentionally executed the greatest thing a batsman can do after a swathe of boundaries: scamper through for one. For some reason, certainly not mathematical, this pleases purists more than another boundary. Compounding matters, the kid then attempted to throw down the stumps at the bowler's end but his throw went so awry that the fieldsman backing up at mid-on was wrong-footed. He slipped on the grass and clumsily fell onto his backside as the ball hurtled past him for four overthrows. Mid-on now lay writhing in agony on the ground, having rolled his ankle in the sorry episode.

On cue, a series of encouraging 'yiews', 'yeahs' and 'save

'ems' rang out from the dressing-room—and one stifled 'FUCK!' from Nuggsy.

Without meaning to, I'd initiated a hell of a counter-punch. I was 15 from three balls, and we were edging back into the match.

Fuck, I'm in here.

I found myself in a moral dilemma. This was, without question, the best start I'd ever had to an innings. Suddenly, I was feeling as if I needed to make the most of the situation. My sense of calm was too good, my clarity unmatched. I turned to the scoreboard to admire my total. Standing underneath it was Dad, alone, striking a familiar pose: slouched against the bricks, arms folded, unmoved, polo shirt tucked into brown Ralph Lauren khaki shorts.

'Yes,' I continued, talking to myself. 'Maybe today's my day. Even *Dad* is here.'

I decided then and there that the fix was off.

Time to really concentrate now. Dad's here. Today's the day.

Their opening quick was now back into the attack. In he came, and I prodded outside off to a half-volley. It caught the edge and was dropped at first slip. I turned to the score-board, where I swear I saw Dad shake his head. I turned a little further towards the pavilion, where I definitely saw Nuggsy nodding his. I just had to concentrate—I was really trying now. I tried to work the next delivery delicately to the on side only to offer a leading edge, the ball lobbing gently in the air between bowler and short cover. The bowler sprawled desperately to catch the ball, but it fell just short of his grasp. I looked towards the scoreboard again to see Dad, now with his back to me, walking from the ground, arms still folded. Just to his right was Nuggsy, flashing two thumbs up, grinning wildly. Christ, he wasn't even trying to conceal his elation any longer.

'That's more like it!' piped the yappy Western Suburbs resident at point.

'Fuck it, the fix is back on.'

'Sorry, mate?' Wizz asked.

We were mid-pitch between overs and I had accidentally mumbled this internal thought out loud.

'Nothing. Sorry, mate. Nothing. Work hard. Just work hard. Singles, etcetera.'

Wizz liked the sound of that—even my use of the word *etcetera*—and presented his glove to punch. Rather than recoil in disgust, as was my normal response to the offer of a glove punch, I executed a frighteningly vigorous right-hand uppercut, which hit him so hard he nearly punched himself in the face. While visibly shaken, Wizz nonetheless appreciated my intensity. He adjusted his glasses and returned to his end.

The onslaught continued, relentless in its ferocity. But as I brought up my 50 with yet another comically brazen slog over mid wicket, I recalled Lara telling me about the 'power of manifestation'. How you have to truly *believe* in something in order for it to come true. Whether it's your career, relationship or whatever, your desires will only manifest if you believe in them wholeheartedly. Perhaps this was the reason that I was failing to get out: because deep down, I truly wanted to succeed. This was the strangest of dark ironies—and the only thing that I knew for sure was that I'd require several months of therapy once this was all over. Eventually I holed out on the boundary, attempting my third successive reverse lap for six. Having bludgeoned 66 runs from just 31 deliveries, I was met with raucous applause as I made my way towards the pavilion—the only exception being Nuggsy, naturally, who attempted to trip me up as I entered the sheds.

We'd finished with a total of 220. Wizz had compiled a neat 47 of his own, but my dashing display had sparked hopes of a stunning victory. As Wizz delivered another rambling five-minute speech, my eyes wandered over to Nuggsy, who was staring daggers in my direction from the other side of the dressing-room. He wasn't even blinking, such was the unflinching intensity of his gaze. As soon as Wizz had finished, Nuggsy leapt from his seat and made his way to the door, beckoning me to follow. We walked around the side of the sheds and behind the decrepit toilet block, safe from prying eyes, to debrief the situation. Clearly, Nuggsy was livid.

'Mate, what the actual fuck were you doing out there? Why now? What are you doing to me?' he fumed.

Flecks of spit flew as he stood over me, his face reddening by the second.

'Nuggsy, mate. I was trying to get out on every single delivery out there,' I whispered.

He looked decidedly unimpressed. I kept going.

'Look, don't make me deconstruct this. Seriously, how many times have you seen me switch hit a first grader for six? It was dumb luck, mate.'

'Well, why did you keep going?' he enquired, quite reasonably. Nuggsy sensed my hesitation. 'Come on, mate, spit it out.'

'I gotta admit that once I was in, I contemplated actually going for it. You know, *trying*. For that, I am sorry. But every time I started trying to score runs, I nearly got out. And every time I tried to get out, I scored runs. It was really fucking depressing.'

Nuggsy shook his head slowly.

'Well, now you've put this whole thing in jeopardy. You were a sure bet to fail, and you've messed it up by not trying. You've managed to fuck up your own dismissal.'

'That's a bit harsh, isn't it, Nuggsy? Are you saying that the only reason you wanted me involved was because you were confident I wouldn't score runs anyway?'

'Yes, mate. That's exactly what I'm saying!'

Inside, I was furious. At first it had seemed that Nuggsy was seeking my help on the basis of friendship—turning to a mate in a time of need—but now it was evident that he'd opportunistically tried to exploit my inevitable failure for monetary gain. Once again, I had mistaken his ruthless pragmatism as endearing vulnerability. Fuck that. Well, it wasn't too late to turn this ship around, was it?

I'd get the ball, and I'd win us this fucking grand final fair and square.

'Well, I'll fix it for you, mate. I promise. Just make sure Wizz gets me the ball and I'll get you the failure you need. The *right* kind of failure this time.'

A faint smile crept over Nuggsy's face. 'Okay, mate. You sure you're not fucking with me?'

'Don't worry, Nuggsy. I'll do a job with the ball for you.'

We both laughed, but for different reasons.

Fuck Nuggsy. Today, I would cement my place in grade cricket history.

'One to start us off here, Nuggsy!' came the call from the cordon.

Nuggsy, a 95-kilo bald man, was wearing a headband today for some reason. His first one was a wide down the leg side, followed by a couple of leaves for no runs. I stood at mid-off, the last to have the ball before giving it to Nuggsy. I'd not said a word to him.

'You all right, champion?' he asked.

'Yes, mate, just focused.'

'Watch this,' Nuggsy said from the corner of his mouth. 'He looks good back and across. This'll be short and wide, and we'll be away.'

Nuggsy came in and placed the ball exactly where he'd hoped. The batsman duly cut hard at the ball, only to nick it safely to our keeper, Spicey, who accepted the catch with glee. The team was joyous; Nuggsy was muted.

'Fucking hell!' Nuggsy growled in the team huddle.

Sensing a few furrowed eyebrows, he hurriedly sought to explain.

'Um, shit ball, that's all. *Shit ball.* How bad was that bloke?'

Then 1-1 became 2 for not many, when their number three scooped a full toss slower ball that slipped to mid-wicket. And so the procession continued. Nuggsy was eventually removed from the attack, after exceeding the number of no balls permitted in a spell, but it didn't halt the tumbling of wickets. Today catches were sticking like they'd never stuck before. The most uncoordinated of teammates were fluking direct-hit run-outs from impossible angles. Eventually the opposition found themselves 9-160 from 35 overs, still 60 runs from victory. We could almost smell the circuit celebration.

'Wizz!' cried Nuggsy. 'How about a bowl for old mate here?' he pointed at me. 'It's his day, after all!'

'Alright, you can have a trundle, mate,' Wizz replied, gesturing for me to warm up.

Two overs passed and I was up. Nuggsy jogged over and took my hat to give it to the umpire, flashing me an evil eye. He looped back to join me as I measured my mark out.

'This is your last chance, champ. I need you to leak 20 here, or else,' he said sternly, like a World War I British general giving his final orders.

'You want 20 runs off one over? Come on, Nuggsy. That's too much. Everyone will know!'

'You know what to do,' he whispered ominously. I could swear he mimicked the motion of slitting my throat as he took up his position at mid-off.

I'd seen Nuggsy be aggressive towards people before— cab drivers, nightclub bouncers, umpires, humble grade cricket scorers—but I'd never really experienced it firsthand. Standing at the top of my mark, I realised that none of this was my fault. That Nuggsy's financial problems were not going to be exacerbated because of me but because of *him*. And now here he was again, just as our team was poised to win a grand final, abusing me while simultaneously insisting

I continue to cheat. I was ropeable at him for placing me in this situation—and ropeable at myself for colluding with it, however badly.

Fuck Nuggsy. I'm going to take this last wicket to win the grand final. This is my time.

I ambled in for my first ball, which was just short of a length outside off, a decent enough pill in anyone's book. Of course, in fitting with the theme of the day, their number eleven batsman skipped down the wicket and dispatched it straight over my head for six. As the ball sailed over the sightscreen, I stole a look at Nuggsy.

'Very nice, mate,' he mouthed silently.

Shit, that was a decent pill.

If that was bad, the second ball was even worse. I attempted to dart one in towards leg stump but over-pitched badly. The same batsman moved inside the line of the ball and allowed his bottom hand to take over, forcefully hoicking it over the deep mid-wicket boundary for yet another six. This truly had become Theatre of the Absurd.

Twelve off two balls.

In I trundled again. Again, a full toss. Again, maximum outcome. How is this happening?

Eighteen off three balls.

At this point, Nuggsy sidled over to put a fatherly arm around me. To all onlookers it would appear that he was consoling me, offering advice on the 'comeback ball', but the reality could not have been more different.

'This is fantastic, mate,' he gushed. 'Keep this up and we're a chance.'

I grabbed the ball off him and nodded weakly.

'In fact, you could even afford to bowl a dot ball now, just so no one gets any ideas,' Nuggsy advised, oblivious to the fact I had been striving to bowl a maiden; striving to be the hero.

Thirty minutes later, there was delirium throughout the ground. As my last delivery sailed over the fence and onto the adjacent highway, the opposition—including dozens of friends, family and club officials—spilled onto the field, waving flags and all sorts of paraphernalia. Some had their pants off, some were calling it the 'greatest comeback in grade cricket history'. I had emerged from my spell having conceded 41 runs from 1.5 overs. Wizz had tried to take me off after my first over, but Nuggsy wouldn't have a bar of it. We lay on the ground, dejected, mystified and mortified at having succumbed this way. All except Nuggsy, that is.

'Unbelievable result, mate! Don't you worry, tonight we'll have one of the great circuits with Bevo and the lads.'

'Bevo and the lads?' I said to him. 'Who the fuck are Bevo's *lads*? Actually, don't answer that.'

I faced Nuggsy squarely, seething with anger. 'Nuggsy, you've cooked me here. You've forced me to cheat against my will, and I did it to help you as a friend. You abused me when you didn't get what you wanted. Match-fixing in grade cricket: it doesn't come grimmer than that, mate. I hope you're happy with your little earner.'

I shoved him in the chest. He was shocked.

'Mate,' I continued. 'We're done. You, me, this, all of this. Fucking done.'

I stormed into the dressing-room. I was done with cricket, and I was done with shit blokes. This was it, seriously.

3

A CHANGE OF PACE

Dad rose from the table, tapping a glass of the menu's second-cheapest red wine, which he held in one hand. That was perhaps the only piece of good advice he'd ever given me in regards to dating: never get the cheapest bottle of wine on the menu—always get the *second* cheapest. I don't really remember anything else from that conversation, or indeed why he was holding court on dating politics and wine to an eleven-year-old boy, but that moment struck me as particularly poignant as he stood at the foot of the table, toasting me with a glass of 2016 Jacob's Creek Shiraz as if it were a 1966 Grange.

'I never thought this day would come,' he began, his deep voice drawing the attention of other diners. 'When your brother finished dux of the school, won the university medal, bought his first house, married Sarah, had his first baby daughter, I remember thinking, on each occasion, "Well, at least your mother and I got *one* of them right!"'

Everyone laughed, including the nearby waiter. In the cold light of day, this was an utter annihilation of my self-esteem and life to this point. But this wasn't the cold light of day; this was a moodily lit Italian restaurant on a Wednesday evening. Bare brick walls and narrow archways kept the warmth in on this cool August evening, while a long-defunct fireplace, now merely ornamental, somehow gave the place a homely feel. The gentle hum of Italian composer Vincenzo Bellini wafted through the speakers to complete the ambience. Dad's words might have been a little harsh, but I'd rarely seen him so happy.

Was Dad proud? Is this what it feels like to have a proud dad?

Channelling his inner *vigneron*, Dad paused to examine his glass of wine, lifting it towards his nose to take a deep sniff before continuing.

'You know, your mother and I had been feeling a little guilty for introducing you to cricket—'

'Amen to that!' my brother chipped in. 'Absolute fucking waste of time!'

'I always thought you were very good, dear,' Mum, sitting next to me, whispered in my ear. That might have been the most condescending thing Mum had ever said, but at least she wasn't asking 'who's winning?'.

Lara squeezed my hand under the table in support. Was Dad about to roast me? Almost definitely.

'And if it wasn't for my knee, we all know I could've made it.'

'You sure could have, Pop! What an athlete!'

I felt like slapping my brother across his face, just like I used to back in the nineties as the physically dominant elder sibling. But puberty had been kinder to him than it had to me and his broad-shouldered, six-foot-four physique intimidated me greatly. Not only had he out-achieved me in life, he'd also won the genetic lottery. Take his eyes, for example. My brother's eyes are not just blue—they are *primary* blue. To this day I've never seen such depth of colour in anyone else's eyes. Then there's the hair. His widow's peak hairline is so aggressive, so strongly defined, so safe from recession that, if anything, it could potentially *secede*, mission-creep past his eyebrows over the course of a lifetime to form an arrow towards his pelvic region; the most alpha thing imaginable, a hairline that points directly at one's own genitals. The hair itself is dark, wavy and slicked back and across into the highly fashionable pompadour style currently favoured by younger, edgier businessmen and creatives. I ran my hand through my own thin, lustreless hair and made a mental note to call Ashley & Martin for a 'free' hair consultation.

While Mum and I shared a certain emotional intelligence and sensitivity, my father and brother were hardcore Type A personalities. As high-achieving, goal-oriented perfectionists, they naturally struggled to understand me as a person. Why was I floating through life, achieving nothing, when I could be negatively gearing my thirteenth property? At the end of the day, I was a 31-year-old man with no university degree, no tangible assets and just $7014 in superannuation spread across six different funds. I wondered, not for the first time, if I was adopted.

'But it began to hurt us. It began to hurt us to see it take so much away from you.'

Mum rolled her eyes. She gripped my arm and leaned over to whisper gently, 'We always knew you'd find the right path.'

Like a seasoned toastmaster, Dad paused for dramatic effect, chuckled softly, and tipped his glass in Lara's direction.

'But then *this* one came along.

'This perfect, angelic, godsend of a girl walked into all of our lives—'

'More like a *charity worker*!' my brother chimed in, his banter declining in quality by the minute.

'Lara,' Dad continued, 'we absolutely adore you. We thank you every single day for helping our eldest son to grow up and move out of the family home. We're now listing his room on Airbnb, so we're financially grateful to you too.'

Here Dad was exaggerating for comic effect—they'd had four guests in eighteen months—but the point was duly made.

'Lara, you are stunning, intelligent, smart, hard-working—'

'Partially blind!' my brother deadpanned. Fuckwit.

'And, well, look where we are today. In my favourite restaurant, drinking this good wine, with all of my family here, including you, Lara. I've got to say, this is one of the proudest days of my life. Congratulations, son.'

I could scarcely believe what I was hearing. All I had done was enrol in a Bachelor of Arts degree at university.

Still, Dad's public admission of pride was a welcome surprise. Normally, he only dealt in curt, clipped statements, rarely more than ten words per sentence. Effusive praise was something he dished out on the rarest of occasions—perhaps when Mum had cooked a particularly delicious meal, or whenever the Reserve Bank chose to drop interest rates, lessening the pressure on his mortgage repayments. For a moment, I wondered whether this toast could potentially lead to a *hug*. But Dad hated public displays of physical affection. These sweet words—and possibly a stiff handshake—would have to do.

In so many ways, the match-fixing incident had been a blessing in disguise. The past eighteen months had given me the chance to address my shortcomings, re-evaluate my priorities, and rediscover my true passions outside of the game of cricket. As such, Tuesday and Thursday training sessions were swapped for night classes at the local TAFE. With gritted teeth and manful resolve, I'd undertaken a Certificate IV in Tertiary Preparation, alongside a host of other mature-age desperates, all trying to put things right. Yes, we were forking out seven hundred bucks for a thirty-six week course on 'how to do your homework', but for us, it was the only way forward. We'd all made our choices.

Tonight, it all seemed so clear. University, graduation, a job, marriage, family—my whole future, all there on the horizon, increasingly within reach. Yes, it was all there to see in that suburban Italian restaurant, which was somewhat fraudulently named Antonio's. I knew for a fact that the owner's name was Gavin.

Meanwhile, my brother continued his heckling.

'You're not going to be one of those annoying mature age students, are you, champ?'

I hadn't expected him to be overtly happy for me. This was pretty much the first evening where we hadn't spent the whole night gushing over his successes. Lara, a psychologist, said she could have written a thousand essays on his selfish introspection and youngest-child syndrome.

'Nah, I'm proud of you, champion. I'm just sorry you couldn't have waited a few more years, so you could have gone to uni with my kids.'

This kind of thing went on for most of the evening. Later I took the opportunity to switch seats as he stepped outside to 'organise an important trade deal', which, given that he worked in corporate sales, I assumed meant 'get a bag'. I guess everyone has their demons, but some are more obvious to others. Kind of like how short people always get bounced, despite the fact they're always good on the short ball. If you just bowled at the stumps, like you would with everyone else, they'd be completely fucked.

But this was the closest, both emotionally and geographically, that I'd been to Dad in years. As I sat alongside him at the dinner table, I cast my mind back to childhood, a young father and son driving to and from cricket matches together. Every Saturday during cricket season we'd cruise endless highways on our way to yet another suburban oval in the middle of nowhere, usually named after an Australian test cricket legend who had no affiliation to the ground whatsoever, except for having once taken his dog for a walk around the outfield before the war. I'd often be too nervous to speak driving to the game, which suited Dad. But on the rare occasions I failed as a junior, Dad's silent disappointment was louder than his six-speed chassis. Even that one time when the gasket blew up on the way home from an under-14 rep final, the explosion wasn't nearly as confronting as the three-hour stretch of silence as we waited for roadside assistance. But our chequered history was all put aside for now. Tonight, I was just a young lad basking in the metaphorical glow of his father's approval. It was more glorious than I had ever imagined.

Fuck, a hug would go down well right now.

'Gavin, another bottle of this Jacob's Creek, my good man!'

There's nothing like a big celebration—be it a family dinner, an engagement party or a wedding—to make you re-evaluate your own relationship.

Lara and I had been together for several years, but it wasn't until Steve and Laura's engagement party that the topic of marriage first arose. Steve and Lara actually used to date back in her university days, but it didn't last because, according to Lara, Steve was 'too big' for her. I always thought that was a strange reason to break up—after all, Steve was only around five-eleven (shorter than me) and in pretty decent shape—but they stayed good friends over the years. At the party, a few people joked about how good Steve and Lara would have been together, how Laura and Lara are really similar names, and how they look almost identical from certain angles (like from front on). For his speech, Steve, a NIDA-trained actor, did this whole bit where he came over to our table and tearfully told Lara she was 'the one that got away'. 'It should have been *you!*' he cried, much to the amusement of all the guests. Anyway, the fallout started on the drive home.

'Laura and Steve haven't even been together as long as we have!' Lara had said, half-joking, but the intent was there.

'You sure? Pretty confident they got together before we did,' I'd tried.

Lara had pressed on. 'They're having a hundred and fifty people to their wedding. Can you believe that? How many would you have at ours?'

'Umm . . . I dunno. Haven't really thought about it.'

'It's all just such a big expense, isn't it? Did you know that the wedding industry is something like 53.4 billion dollars in the States?'

This had struck me as being the female equivalent of knowing your teammate's batting average to the second decimal place. As always, the important thing to do is use the words *something*, *like*, *about* or *roughly* before citing a trivial fact with autistic accuracy.

The conversation stopped there, but over the months that followed I'd been thinking more and more about our future together. Tonight's dinner had been a complete success, and a new life awaited me. For so long, I'd actively avoided any form of personal development that didn't directly relate to cricket, but now I had the chance to make up for that lost time. Was *marriage* part of this equation? I thought back to all the blokes I used to play grade cricket with. Dazza was married and divorced before the age of thirty. Last time I'd seen him he was contemplating 'doing the right thing' and popping the question to a bird he'd impregnated after a night out on the circuit. Robbo used to flippantly refer to his wife as the 'misso'—'Got to get home before the misso cracks the shits,' he'd say after draining his seventh beer in the sheds inside an hour. I was surprised to later find out that his wife, Lindsay, was actually an accomplished criminal barrister. Others, like Wippa and Haynesy, had long-suffering wives and children waiting for them somewhere. If only those children were old enough to know that Daddy would rather stand at second slip and touch the cricket ball twice in six hours than spend a beautiful Saturday afternoon teaching them to read. All up, I'd assessed that 'grade cricket' and 'marriage' were essentially incompatible constructs. But now, freed from the burdens of grade cricket—and with an exciting new path ahead of me—perhaps the time was right to call Mr Henderson and ask for his daughter's hand—or whatever the fuck the protocol was these days regarding marriage proposals.

'Water or gum?' the Uber driver asked as we hopped into the car.

I accepted the offer of a Mount Franklin and buckled in for the ride, my arm tucked around Lara, who'd shifted into the adjacent middle seat. Without any prompting whatsoever, Shaun—our thirty-something driver—began telling us his entire education and employment history, which included a law degree (honours), a seven-year stint at a multinational law firm, and a half-finished MBA. Like all Uber drivers, Shaun was suspiciously over-qualified to be picking up a thirteen-dollar fare at 10.50 p.m. on a Wednesday evening. I zoned out and contemplated my future, a smile across my face.

I won't bore you too much with the details of my own job other than to say I sell various products and services for a living. I have a meagre base salary of $55,000 (gross), which comes out to $44,653 once you deduct the tax. Precisely $5225 of my gross income goes into a superannuation fund (I don't even know which one). I pay $1500 per month in rent for the apartment I share with Lara (she pays $2500 a month), so I'm forking out around $18,000 a year towards some bloke's mortgage. Once you deduct a year's worth of utilities ($2400—probably more than that, actually, considering the way electricity prices are going in this state), there's about $24,000 of disposable income left over, which comes out to $2000 a month. Occasionally, when I somehow manage to close a deal, I'll earn a commission cheque, in which case I'll enjoy a momentary boost of serotonin, and perhaps a fleeting sense of purpose. I may even take Lara out for brunch and treat her to a plate of smashed avocado and feta, her favourite meal. Hitting your monthly commission is like a nice-looking 30-odd in cricket: it makes you feel good for a day or two, but it isn't going to allow you to outbid cashed-up Chinese investors at a high-stakes property auction.

Perhaps it was the four glasses of red wine talking but I immediately resolved to quit my dead-end job and focus on carving a new path for myself. I could pick up a part-time job making coffees, labouring—whatever, it didn't matter. What mattered, ultimately, was my happiness. I reached into my pocket, pulled out my iPhone and drafted a letter of resignation in my Notes app.

> Hi Pat,
>
> I wanted you to know that I've decided to enrol in university and pursue a new direction. As such, I am officially resigning from my position effective as of the end of this month.
>
> It's been a pleasure working with you, and please let me know what to expect in terms of accrued leave time and my final pay cheque.

I hesitated for a second. Was this the right thing to do? I could probably figure out an arrangement where I could come in one or two days a week around uni if I really wanted to. But the winds of change were in the air, and without the burden of this terrible job, my future seemed so much brighter. With the emotional (and financial) support of Lara, I could harness all my energy into university.

Fuck it. I'm doing it.

I copied and pasted the draft letter into a text message to Pat, scanning it quickly for typos. Satisfied, I pressed send before turning my phone off and stuffing it back into my jeans pocket, breathing a sigh of relief. Done. Meanwhile, Lara began to stir just as Shaun pulled into the driveway of our apartment complex.

'Did I fall asleep?'

'Only for a bit.'

'Red wine always knocks me out,' she said, completing the sentence with a yawn. 'I think I'm going to go straight to bed.'

'No worries. I might stay up for a bit.'

I collapsed on the couch and opened up the iPad, planning to catch up on the latest episode of *Billions*. I punched in the passcode, but after two failed attempts, I finally realised I'd picked up Lara's work iPad and not my own.

'What's the code for your iPad again?' I called out to Lara, who was in the bathroom, doing whatever it is that happens in there after a night out.

'Same as your career batting average, remember?' she called back.

So, 11.64. I could have married her there and then.

I unlocked the iPad and clicked on a tab to open up Stan, only to be taken straight to her Gmail account. I was not intending to pry (Lara often described trust as the most important part of any relationship) but an email was open that demanded my immediate attention.

Subject: Re: Guatemala Volunteer Program
From: rikki_borowitz@guatemalachildren.org
To: autumnmarie89@hotmail.com; joerichardson@aol.com; zacfrasersmith@hotmail.com; kaichristian69@gmail.com . . . and 10 more

Hello Everyone,
Hope you're all doing well as we get ready to begin our planning and training for the vacation programs.

This week has already been somewhat hectic, as most transitions are, but I am really looking forward to seeing everyone together on Skype next Friday afternoon. Your input, energy and ideas are what will make this project successful!

I won't write a lot right now, but I do want to add two very important things. First—we just want to send a ton of appreciation to each of you. We know the effort and sacrifice that it takes to come to Guatemala and do the work that you are about to do. The successes that you find will come mostly in baby steps, and that is normal and to be expected. Yet, when you look back and see what you have accomplished together, you will have many reasons to feel proud and happy.

And second—the idea behind what we are planning to work on is much more than academic enrichment and some fun and games. It's about giving children a chance to make good choices, to work collaboratively, to solve problems creatively and to think for themselves.

Again, many thanks to each of you—and I look forward to meeting you all in person very soon!

xo

I forced myself to read the email several times in order to take it all in. At first I wasn't sure what I was looking at. Was this a cruel hoax? Was someone having a laugh at my expense? I thought back to the time Damo got arrested for the Nigerian Prince bank scam he'd been running from his Hotmail account. Over the course of three months, dozens of unsuspecting pensioners had transferred thousands of dollars into the account of 'Reverend Father August Goodluck' (aka Damo's Flexi Saver bank account). Reverend Goodluck was set to inherit the princely sum of US$2.5 million but simply needed some assistance in paying taxes to help transfer the money. The Australian

Federal Police turned up to our game and dragged Damo kicking and screaming from the pitch (he was on 30-odd at the time, and looking in good nick). He ended up serving an eighteen-month sentence, but the biggest crime in my eyes was the AFP's decision to arrest a bloke well on his way to triple figures.

But no. This was real. I dug deeper into the email chain, which tragically revealed that Lara had been corresponding with this volunteer coordinator for the past two months in order to secure a six-month placement in Guatemala. I scrolled through random sentences and phrases from Lara that will stick with me forever.

'I can't wait to get over there!'

'Looking forward to starting a new chapter!'

'Thank you so much for this opportunity!'

Suddenly Lara walked out of the bedroom to grab some water, half-asleep. Trembling with silent rage, I couldn't help myself.

'Lara, what have you done?' I whispered.

'What are you talking about?' she answered mid-yawn, bleary-eyed.

'Um, when were you going to tell me about Guatemala?'

Lara stopped still; her expression turned to one of shock, she was now wide awake.

'Wait . . . have you been reading my *emails*?'

I was becoming angry, indignant.

'Well, your Gmail account was open—the email just popped up. Anyway, you're going to Guatemala and you weren't even going to tell me?'

'No, I mean . . . of course I was going to tell you . . .'

'Lara, I can't believe you could do this,' I intervened, seizing the opportunity to play the victim.

'Wait, we talked about this six months ago, remember? You said you weren't interested in travelling to Central America and learning Spanish.'

I genuinely couldn't recall the conversation, but didn't want to admit to it. Like a batsman feathering one through to the keeper, I gamely stood my ground.

'Lara, you're being selfish.'

'No, I'm going over there to help educate orphans . . .'

A few moments passed, allowing for both parties to calm down and step outside the situation. We went back and forth for a while as I tried to understand her motivation, exchanging barbs across the room as each side made their case. Eventually Lara took a deep breath, walked slowly over and placed a hand on my shoulder.

'Look, I think we're just in different places right now.'

'What do you mean?'

'Well, you're off to university soon—and that's great, I'm really happy for you—but you know I've been working for the past ten years straight. I really need a break. You know that I've always wanted to go backpacking . . .'

This was true. For years Lara had pined to strap a backpack on and see the world, but the constraints of full-time work—and being in a romantic relationship with a grade cricketer—had made that somewhat difficult. Our occasional holidays had always revolved around my cricketing schedule. April was usually the time we'd go somewhere; the team rarely ever made the finals. But ever since we'd watched the movie *Eat Pray Love* together on the night of her thirtieth birthday, she'd developed a burgeoning interest in travel and spirituality. Our bookshelf, once filled with Penguin classics and psychology textbooks, was now home to dozens of travel-lit novels (Mark Twain's *Roughing It*, Jack Kerouac's *On the Road*), not to mention various new-age self-help books by the likes of Eckhart Tolle and co. I should have noticed the signs, but I've never been able to read a wrong 'un delivery, let alone a woman. I knew Eckhart Tolle had written a lot about karma. Was *this* karma? Instead of patronising Lara for her morning meditation classes and Bikram yoga sessions, I should have been there alongside her. God knows my rig could have used the workout.

Mere hours ago, Dad had made an uncharacteristically emotional toast to Lara, calling her part of the family and 'our future daughter-in-law.' She had accepted the praise with discernible embarrassment, which I'd initially taken at face value. Now I realised her uncharacteristic lack of eye contact during the dinner was probably because she knew the end was near. But despite the shock factor, I was surprised at how calm I felt. With the world at my feet, perhaps now was the time to step back out and reclaim my youth, my independence, my manhood. Was Lara giving me an out here? Better to end things now than five or ten years down the road, like Dazza, spending a mountain in court fees, seeing your kids once every three weeks.

'So . . . is this the end?' I managed.

We looked at each other, tears rolling freely down our cheeks, and hugged, a final, lengthy embrace.

We lay side by side in the same bed that night, but everything had changed. And in the morning, I was on my own again.

4

MOVING IN

There's a popular saying that cricket is a real 'leveller'. The thing about cricket is that you can score a chanceless hundred one week and be the toast of your cricket club, only to turn up next week on a 42-degree day and get an absolute jaffa first ball, a send-off from a sixteen-year-old and a ticket for parking in a designated clearway. Now cricket is really hard again. You're second-guessing everything. The ball, bigger than a watermelon when you were in form, now resembles a peppermint Tic Tac. A 43-year-old part-time off spinner nicknamed Bludger with a body mass index of 37 has you in all sorts at Tuesday night's training session, your teammates rolling on the ground in hysterics as he traps you in front with yet another of his infamous 'nudes'.

Emotionally shattered and lacking confidence in your ability, you turn up next Saturday and it's like you've completely forgotten how to bat. Basically, you've had a cricket lobotomy. The opposition senses it and promptly unleashes the most cutting and on-point sledging you've ever received in your career, targeting your weakest spots like an experienced second speaker in a high-school debate. You spoon one to cover just to get the fuck out of there, and six weeks later you're openly threatening to give the game away, having copped five successive ducks (all dubious LBWs adjudicated by a different octogenarian umpire) on beautiful sunny weekends.

In short, the very moment you think you're on top, cricket—much like life—has a way of bringing you back down to earth with shattering force.

Up until now, I had been sharing a modern two-bedroom apartment with my de facto partner. Our apartment was located in the 'cool' part of town, an energetic, vibrant melting pot of racial diversity and left-wing politics, dozens of lively bars, cafes and live music venues all within walking distance. But in the space of twenty-four hours my world had changed entirely. I was back living with my parents in the deepest bowels of suburbia, surrounded by white, semi-retired baby boomers with centre-right political leanings. I had impulsively resigned from my job too, so I was effectively unemployed. I had to take three different buses just to get into the city. Even the nearest cafe was a fifteen-minute walk away, but there wasn't any point: the coffee was Vittoria and they didn't even serve smashed avocado. Yuck, indeed.

Walking into my old room for the first time after the break-up, I was greeted by three perfectly folded fresh towels on my single bed. At least Mum was happy to have me home again. I wasn't sure whether this was simply Airbnb protocol and she was keen to keep her five-star host rating, but either way it was nice to feel welcomed. A carafe of water sat on the bedside table, alongside a notepad with suggestions on 'things to do during your stay in the area'. Naturally, all my childhood relics had been removed in favour of a minimalist interior. My favourite poster, a shot of Mark Waugh playing a slashing square cut in a test match against the West Indies, had been replaced with a tasteful white canvas featuring a stencil print of a sailing boat. Another poster, of Glenn McGrath, wrist cocked as he launched into his inimitable gather, resplendent in a 1997/98 lightning bolt era 'Limited Overs' strip (they weren't called ODIs back then), had been traded for an elegant vine-themed wall decal, which stretched all the way across to the bedroom door.

I had to admit, the room looked good. A fresh coat of pristine white paint had livened it up dramatically. I couldn't even tell you what colour the bedroom walls were before, since every inch of space had been taken up with posters of my cricketing idols. My shelves, too, bustled with trophies in various shades of gold, silver and bronze, all symbols of my youthful dominance. *U10 Jackson Shield Player of the Year. U12 Batting Average Award. U14 Representative Player of the Series.* My name engraved on all of them. A framed scorecard of my maiden century rested on the lower shelf. In dark times I would walk over and study this glorious innings in detail, savouring the pencil lines for every run scored. Yes, girls thought I was weird, and I certainly wasn't going anywhere academically, but at least I was good at *cricket*. But as part of Mum's renovation rampage, this sturdy wooden bookshelf filled with trophies had been replaced with a DIY space-saving floating wall shelf, each level stocked with framed pictures featuring inspirational quotes. The bottom level boasted colourful letter blocks that had been arranged into the word 'LOVE'—something I had never been able to extract from my father, yet apparently was in ample supply for our Airbnb guests.

The incident with Nuggsy had left me sickened with cricket, and keen to purge myself of all such paraphernalia. I had even gone so far as to list my cricket kit on eBay, but sadly there were no bidders (even at the Buy It Now price of fifteen dollars). As such, I'd taken it over to my parents' house, stuffed it in the closet and forgotten all about it. I wondered whether it, too, had failed to survive Mum's Airbnb makeover. For a second I feared it had been taken to the local St Vincent de Paul's charity shop and sold for a fiver to some impressionable kid who just made the worst decision of his life, the cycle set to continue—another young life ruined.

With some trepidation, I walked over to the cupboard and pulled aside a curtain of hanging clothes. Yes, there it was, my old kit, all alone in the dark, sad and neglected. The final vestige of my cricketing past. It seemed to have shrunk in size over the last eighteen months, perhaps wilting from a lack of natural light. A funereal gloom overwhelmed me as I looked at the kit there, lifeless in the shadows. The word 'coffin' sprang to mind. I had always found it strange that cricketers ironically referred to their kit as a 'coffin'.

I guess, if nothing else, it's an insight into the dark, twisted minds of cricketers. There's no doubting that something had died in that kit, and it wasn't just the mouldy banana that had been there for the past eighteen months. My cricketing dreams, specifically, had died in that kit.

I slammed the cupboard shut as a shiver ran through my body. It was only 5.30 p.m., but I went straight to bed.

While Mum was pleased to welcome me back into the family home, Dad was barely able to mask his disappointment. Back in my youth, Dad was a largely invisible presence in the household, having spent forty-plus years working in the financial services industry, mostly in middle management. But now that he was retired, he was just constantly around. Like all men of that age who've spent the majority of their lifetime in the workforce, he still vigilantly maintained, well into retirement, the same morning routine he'd employed throughout his career. He'd wake up at 5.45 a.m., have a shower and a shave, walk down to the yard and fetch the newspapers, then return to the kitchen to prepare his breakfast: warm oats with three-quarters of a banana and a dash of brown sugar. For someone lucky enough to have avoided serving in Vietnam due to a 'hernia', he placed a military-like emphasis on routine. For the rest of the day he would loiter around the house, moving photo frames one inch to the right, cleaning the leaves out of the gutter twice a day, re-reading the *Financial Review* from front to back.

I walked into the kitchen that following morning and there he was, silently thumbing through the pages of the *Fin*.

'Morning, Dad,' I managed upon entering.

'BHP down 2.5 per cent,' he mumbled to himself.

Did he not hear me?

I tried again. 'Up to much today?'

He flicked a page and whistled through his teeth.

'Looks like there's going to be another rate rise,' he stated, whistling through his teeth, again, to no one.

I stuck two slices of Helga's bread into the toaster, pushing the lever down. Dad lowered his paper momentarily and studied me quizzically from head to toe.

'Still in your pyjamas? It's 8.30 a.m.'

Yes, I was still in my pyjamas, but in my defence, I was still wallowing from my terrible break-up with Lara.

Dad carried on. 'You going to get a job?'

'Well, I'm looking f—'

'When I was your age, I already had fifteen years of full-time work under my belt.'

During conversations like these, I always consoled myself with the fact that my parents' generation was responsible for the majority of the social and economic problems that exist today. Born in the aftermath of World War II, they were lucky enough to be the beneficiaries of free higher education, affordable house prices and a stable global outlook. It seemed like there were jobs everywhere back then too. By the sounds of it, you could walk into any office and ask, 'Can I have a job?', no references required, nothing. That was literally how everyone got work back then. You'd shake some bloke's hand and, over the course of several decades, eventually work your way up the corporate ladder to become the CEO. Some forty years later you announce your retirement, having racked up enough superannuation to purchase three waterfront properties in Sydney. These days, if you walked into an office and just point-blank asked for a job, you'd be escorted out by security within six seconds on suspicion of being an Islamic State terrorist. As such, we're all stuck doing three-month unpaid internships on the off-chance we might snare a $35,000 per annum content-writing gig for some shitty youth-skewed online publication.

'Dad, you have no idea what it's like to grow up in this era of global insecurity. Your generation had it so easy. Free education. Cheap housing . . .'

'Well, we're paying for your university tuition, so it's still free for you, dickhead,' he barked. 'You know, your brother had an academic scholarship—everything fully paid for. Now, he's director of sales for APAC at MilTrix . . .'

In my defence, being an adult *is* fucking tough these days—much tougher than it used to be. And even if you are able to get a decent job, good luck buying property. A recent study showed that Australian millennials rank second-last for home ownership, with the United Arab Emirates bringing up the rear. In China and Mexico, for example, seventy per cent of young adults own a home. Sure, the pollution in Beijing might cut your life expectancy by fifteen years, but at least you're able to get into the housing market early. Here in Australia, even if you *are* able to put a deposit on a cute little studio apartment going for $1.4 million, situated next to the airport with no natural light, just the slightest interest rate increase will leave you financially crippled for the rest of your natural life. And then there's stagnant wage growth, a slowing Chinese economy and various other macroeconomic factors that I don't really understand (yet will claim to be an expert on after three glasses of wine), which mean that my chances of buying property are about as good as me holding onto a catch in the cordon: fucking slim to none.

Dad sighed. 'What do you want to do with your life, mate?'

'I don't know. I want to get this degree and then . . . I'm not sure. I want to be a writer. Maybe I can get into journalism . . .'

'Journalism? That's a dying industry, champ. What else can you do with an Arts degree?'

Fuck, that's a hard one to answer, isn't it? My silence only encouraged Dad to press forth with greater vigour.

'Anyway, we're forking out of our retirement fund to pay for this degree. You better make the most of it.'

And with that, Dad rose from the table, took his dish to the sink, washed it dutifully and shuffled out of the room.

Fuck, this was going to be a testing little period.

I often say it was grade cricket that first exposed me to the strange behaviours of men within a closed environment, but, in reality, it began much earlier than that.

Dad has hosted a regular poker night for as long as I can remember. When I say *regular*, I should specify that Dad has held a poker night on the second Thursday of every month for the past thirty-five years straight. Growing up, I can still remember how Dad's behaviour changed on poker night. In fact, it was like he was a different man entirely. Once a month, he would arrive home in an unusually cheerful mood, a case of beer under his arm, offer Mum a quick kiss on the cheek, and hurry downstairs to stock the bar fridge and set up the table. Around 7 p.m. the guests would arrive, all stocky, grey-haired, married heterosexuals in their forties and fifties, with monosyllabic names like Rick, Don, Bob and Ray. On their way through they'd attempt some low-level flirtation with Mum, and ruffle my hair affectionately—*How's school going, big guy? Hit any runs last weekend?*—before making their way downstairs to join Dad in the so-called 'function room' (aka the basement).

For Dad, this was his one night of the month to let his hair down (what was left of it) and relax over a few beers and some banter. Naturally, this was a strictly all-male affair. While Mum was the official cook for the evening—charged with ensuring the party pies were heated to perfection— she was forbidden from attending the function. And with good reason, for the chat that took place in this room was not for delicate ears. I remained upstairs in the TV room, trying valiantly to overhear the content of these muffled conversations. Every now and then, a veritable explosion of deep-throated laughter would erupt from downstairs and carry on for several minutes, followed by the endless chinking of glasses and ice cubes rattling around in whisky tumblers: a symphony of manhood. Yes, it was the early

1990s, and it was certainly a great time to be a white hetero-sexual man in Australia.

After a couple of hours, Dad, six or seven beers deep by this stage, would come upstairs and invite me down to talk about my cricket. He'd sit back proudly as I confidently discussed my burgeoning career, leaving all in no doubt that this precocious young talent would represent Australia some day. I loved being invited into that smoky cellar room; loved being privy to this secret men's business; loved that Dad was proud of me. I'd be allowed to stick around past my bedtime on the condition that I freshen the guests' glasses upon request (sidenote: I learned how to make an Old Fashioned cocktail at the age of seven). For the rest of the evening I'd sit there silently, picking at salted peanuts and listening to their exaggerated stories of corporate triumph and historic sexual conquest. In retrospect, poker night was little more than an opportunity for these men to escape their families and participate in several hours' worth of drinking and gambling, which isn't that far removed from grade cricket when you think about it. But, boy, what a time they were having. To my young eyes, this right here was the pinnacle of adulthood. This was where I wanted to be when I grew up.

Anyway, I'd forgotten that Dad's regular poker night was still a thing until the second Thursday rolled around.

'Just make yourself scarce,' Dad had firmly instructed me that morning. 'I haven't told anyone that you're back living here.'

I felt the bedroom was probably going to be my best option. There I'd be safe from any potentially awkward conversations about how my life was going—or worse, how my *cricket* was going. At 7 p.m. on the dot, I heard the men arrive and make their way to the basement, trampling down the stairs like a herd of rowdy elephants.

I was half asleep when my bedroom door opened and in lurched a bloated sixty-something man grappling awkwardly with his fly.

God, what the fuck is going on here?

'Oh . . . this isn't the bathroom,' Rick McGuinness mumbled quietly to himself.

Rick was Dad's best mate from high school, and the best man at his wedding all those years back. He'd been coming to this house every second Thursday for the past thirty-five years yet had forgotten where the bathroom was situated. This could have been an honest mistake, or more likely due to the nine full-strength beverages he'd consumed in the space of two hours. Either way, I lay still, hoping he hadn't seen me, keen to avoid an awkward encounter.

As he was turning to leave, Rick's eyes surveyed the room briefly before eventually landing on me. He squinted for a moment, as if doing a mental calculation, before flashing a big toothy grin, like his Powerball numbers had just come up.

'G'day, champion! Gee, I haven't seen you in . . . it must be ten or fifteen years!'

'Oh hi, Mr McGuinness,' I managed. 'How are you?'

'Good, good. Are you living back at home now?'

'Yeah, I am, actually. I mean, not for long, though. How's Jason?'

'Ah, Jason's just had another kid—a boy. He and Belinda just closed the deal on their second property up in the Hunter. Do you guys keep in touch? I know he was a couple of years behind you at school . . .'

'No, we haven't, actually. Say hi for me.'

Rick lingered in the doorway for a few moments longer.

'Look, I've just got to go and drain the main vein, but you should come down with us for a bit of poker, yeah? You're an adult now and it's been a long time, so we should have a beer. Plus, the other blokes would be thrilled to see you.'

'Sorry, Rick, but Dad really doesn't want me to interrupt the poker night. In fact, he told me to make myself scarce . . .'

'Rubbish, don't worry about that old bastard! You're coming with me,' he ordered. 'Now, just hang on a moment while I empty my dick.'

The paper-thin walls proved an insufficient sound barrier as Rick's thick flow of urine splashed down on the toilet water with serious velocity, no doubt spilling onto the porcelain seat, which he wouldn't have bothered to put up. He let out a long, deep sigh as three litres of alcohol departed his body, before flushing the toilet (a small win for hygiene) and coming back into the room without washing his hands (immediately negating the win).

'Let's go, champion.'

'Hang on, let me j—'

'Nah, come on, get moving!'

I was certain this was a terrible idea, but Rick just wouldn't take no for an answer. It made me wonder whether there was something to that rape accusation levelled at him by a former employee. Anyway, he ushered me downstairs, flung the door open and pushed me in. There I stood, a 31-year-old man-child in a floral dressing gown, before six tipsy white blokes in their sixties.

'Gentlemen, look who I found!'

A loud cheer filled the room.

'Here he is! It's the big fella!'

I smiled weakly, shrugging my shoulders. Dad looked mortified.

'I remember when you were just a young kid—I think you were playing metropolitan under 14s. Are you still playing?' Don, a property law barrister, asked earnestly.

'No, I don't play anymore,' I replied politely, stealing another glance at Dad.

'Well, you got further than your old man ever did!' Rick grinned, cocking one eye at Dad.

A couple of the other gentlemen joined in to give Dad a good old-fashioned ribbing, as blokes do.

'Seriously, mate, you were a *terrible* cricketer!' Rick roared, to great laughter.

My whole life, I'd been fed the story that Dad was an exceptionally talented cricketer who could have made it all the way, if not for doing his knee in an unfortunate skiing incident. I bookmarked this fresh development for a later date. Meanwhile, Rick helpfully brought a chair around to the head of the table and placed a fresh premium beer in front of me.

'Take a seat here, son! We dealing you in?'

I hadn't actually played poker since grade cricket. Every grade cricket club worth its salt has an annual 'poker night', which presents a formalised opportunity to mingle with your cricket mates and guzzle copious amounts of alcohol, free from the judgemental eyes of your partner and family. Generally the event is held in the club pavilion, with a topless waitress providing refreshments on command for roughly two hundred dollars an hour (I know the rates due to my time serving on the social committee for a couple of years back in the mid-2000s). The lady in question is usually accosted by at least one sexually frustrated club desperate who tries to talk to her about her job. I still remember when Joffo, approximately thirteen beers deep, tried to tell one of the waitresses that he could 'save you from all this'. His offer was politely declined as Joffo, a 37-year-old divorced father of two with a negative credit history and a serious alcohol problem, was in no position to be anyone's saviour. But while I was never a big fan of these events, I did know they were critically important for fledgling players who wished to ingratiate themselves with the key figures at the club. In terms of establishing and maintaining social capital, atten- dance at the club poker night was essential. Even if you were yet to suffer from a debilitating gambling addiction, it helped to at least appear as if you did. After all, everyone's suspicious of a cleanskin.

'Come on, mate, you in?'

I snapped back into the present to realise Dad's mates were chanting, banging their fists on the round table to maintain a percussive beat. It was like I was back in a grade cricket dressing-room again, Nuggsy smashing a stump against a rubbish bin to provide some semblance of rhythm to our victory song. *Why was there always a Sulo rubbish bin in every grade cricket dressing-room?* I've always been particularly susceptible to peer pressure. Get a good rhythmic chant going and it doesn't matter what you're trying to get me to do, I'll probably do it. If Nuggsy killed a backpacker for some reason, I'd probably help him bury the body if he got a good chant going.

'Take a seat! Take a seat! TAKE A SEAT!'

I sat down at the table. More cheers erupted. It was as if I was pounding glasses of *soju* with a room full of Korean businessmen. Endless cheering. If this was a grade cricket situation, these cheering sounds would be replaced with high-pitched 'yiews', but the sentiment was the same, even if the sounds were more guttural. My seat was located directly opposite Dad. He sat there shuffling the cards, a sinister smile on his face, channelling a Bond villain. I couldn't help but admire his shuffling technique as he dexterously flipped the cards from hand to hand, exhibiting exceptional control. The fast-moving cards sounded like crisp bills flicking through a money-counting machine.

'Mate, you'll have to buy in to be a part of this,' Dad said smugly. 'So what are you going to put in the kitty?'

I looked at the middle of the table. There were thousands of dollars there. Crisp, gorgeous-looking fifty-dollar bills, seemingly *hundreds* of them. More money than I had ever dreamed of winning. I thought about my own meagre bank balance; last time I'd checked I had $37.04 in my savings account. It had actually been months since I'd checked my balance (I'd always urgently press 'no balance required' whenever I went to the ATM because I just didn't want to know), but regardless, I certainly didn't have any spare fifty-dollar notes in my bathroom robe to nonchalantly chuck into the kitty.

'Umm, I don't have any money on me, Dad.'

'Hang on, I'll buy you in, champion!' Rick spluttered, reaching into his pocket to produce a fistful of bills.

He didn't even bother to count them, just flung them into the general vicinity of the kitty. We all watched as they fanned out across the table. It was a real baller move, and one that provoked yet another positive vocal reaction from the now very well-lubricated guests.

'Fuck, who cares about money—plenty more where that came from!' Rick yelled, to more laughter.

The throaty guffaws reverberated around the poorly insulated basement and out across the street. I heard a dog bark in the distance, then another one. Rick's *Wolf of Wall Street* hedonism had triggered a chain reaction across the otherwise silent neighbourhood.

'Alright, boys,' Dad said after the noise had finally subsided. 'Final round of the night—winner takes all.'

'Ooooooooooooooh,' the men whispered in unison.

On cue, everyone threw their money into the centre of the table. The scene resembled a mid-2000s Ja Rule film clip all of a sudden, except here, the actors were old white Australian men with a combined property portfolio exceeding $40 million and a natural aversion to contemporary African-American rap music.

Dad dealt the cards out with a flourish. I picked my two up and took a peek. They were grim: a two of diamonds and a seven of clubs. I knew that my only option was to bluff.

Thankfully, grade cricket had been wonderful training in brazen deception.

'We going large, champion?' Rick asked.

Everyone to him was a 'champion'. I genuinely wondered how on earth he had managed to scale the corporate ladder to join the executive leadership team at one of Australia's big four banks when his vocabulary was so blatantly limited.

Dad took a moment to compose himself. Slowly, purposefully, he removed his watch from his left wrist and placed it on the table in front of him.

'Lads, this watch was given to me by Bill Craig back in 1985, when I helped close the biggest deal of my career.'

'Ah, the Belle-Pentley merger. How's Craigy going, anyway?' Don asked.

'He passed away last year, mate.'

All six men raised a silent glass to Craigy, whoever the fuck he was.

'*Vale!*'

Dad kissed the watch tenderly before leaning over to place it on top of the pile of money, where it sat rather incongruously. He paused for the full effect before taking a generous swig of his whisky.

'All in.'

More cheers. I looked at my cards. They hadn't changed. Still shit.

'So, you in, or are you out?' Bob Ringland asked. It hadn't gone unnoticed that these were Bob's first words for the evening. Presumably the official rare unit of the group.

'This bloke's got *nothing!*' Dad shouted, to guffaws of laughter.

Dad was right. This hand was diabolically shithouse. But, to my advantage I had nothing to lose, except for the mountain of money that Rick had stumped up to buy me in.

'Dad, I want to be in . . . but I'm out of coin.'

'Well, you can't just say that, mate. You've got to put something on the table if you want to buy in. I just put Craigy's watch in. What have you got on you?'

I looked at Rick, who shrugged apologetically.

'Sorry, mate, I'm out of coin too. How about that robe of yours?' he joked. At least I hoped he was joking.

Fuck. I really needed that money. My mind went into overdrive, the most it had worked in years. What could I offer instead? Dad, after all, had everything. He was a man in his late sixties with a reasonable stock portfolio, two wholly-owned properties and plenty saved up in super (even after the global financial crisis 'took half of it'). There was nothing I could give to him that would be of any tangible value.

'Dad, I'll mow the lawns once a month for the next ten years.'

The room broke into laughter. Hooting, hysterical laughter.

Dad waited for the room to calm down before cracking a crooked half-smile.

'Mate, that's not good enough.'

'I'll make you breakfast every morning.'

'No, that's not going to cut it either.'

I gulped and took yet another deep breath, inhaling Don's second-hand cigar smoke in the process. It was time to bring out the big guns.

'Dad,' I hesitated. 'I . . . I promise to finally get my act together and sort my life out.'

Dad put his glass down. 'Hang on, are you serious?'

'Yep. First thing tomorrow I'll go and look for a part-time job. I'll also get on Gumtree and try to find a room.'

Dad paused theatrically and scratched his chin. 'Okay.'

A chorus of whispered apprehension came from the onlookers.

It was over pretty quickly from there. With very little fanfare, Dad threw his cards down to reveal a pair of aces. When added to the two aces that were already on the table, Dad effectively held a quartet of aces. I don't know what the actual term for that is, but to my uneducated eyes it seemed like a fucking good hand.

'And you?'

I felt my face getting red. Time to make a dignified exit. Well, as dignified an exit as one can make in a floral dressing gown.

'Look at him go! Pack 'em, boy!' Dad hollered, eyes ablaze, as I rose to leave the room.

I quickly scampered from the scene, their hoots and hollers chasing me all the way up the staircase and into my dreams.

I've heard about how difficult it is for a widow or widower to continue living in the house they once shared with their life partner. Everywhere they look, they see memories. The chair that Alfred used to sit in on Sunday afternoons. The wallpaper Marjorie chose after six months of deliberation. It was the same for me too: everywhere I looked in this house I saw *cricket*. The backyard lawn had been concreted over a couple of years ago, but I could still visualise my famous 378 not out against my brother on Boxing Day 1997. The faint muddy tennis ball marks on the side of the house reminded me of the countless hours I spent working on my front foot press after school. Little trigger points everywhere.

Fresh from an indulgent and highly unnecessary afternoon nap, I eyed the cupboard across the room. I'd been thinking about my cricket kit ever since I'd moved home but hadn't revisited the cupboard since that first day. I glanced at my watch—still thirty minutes until dinner. In my dreamy, trancelike state, I got out of bed and opened the cupboard to free my kit from the darkness, slowly unzipping the dusty bag to peek inside. Within milliseconds, a familiar waft greeted me. The powerful yet intoxicating brew of mouldy banana, fifty-plus sunscreen and crusty, sweat-laden gear was like a bearhug from a long-lost relative. My grade cricket cap was there on the top, a sweat streak running across the base of the brim. What happened next I can't really explain, other than to say my natural instincts took over. It just felt right.

I kneeled down to put my left pad on first, just I had done every innings since the age of ten; even here in my bedroom, with nothing on the line, superstitious habits took over. I'd hit my first 50 at the age of eleven after putting my left pad on first and I'd done it religiously every match ever since. Statistically speaking, it had no bearing on my performance (I averaged 11.34 over my entire career, according to those lying pricks at MyCricket) but it gave me a false sense of comfort and confidence. Not sure if it's related but I also turn the light on and off thirty-seven times before I go to bed every night.

The pads weren't enough, though. For realism, I decided to wear my gloves, thigh pad, armguard and helmet, too. There I stood, in front of the full-length mirror, completely naked, save for my cricket equipment. There was only one key item missing from my ensemble: the bat, the *pièce de résistance*. I had two cricket bats in my kit, as all half-decent amateur cricketers do. One was an old Gray-Nicolls that had been gifted to me by a former state player. By 'gifted' I mean that he'd chucked it into the bushes after a particularly awful net session, loudly proclaiming it to be a 'fucked stick'. I'd waited until the end of training before venturing into the thick undergrowth and collecting the prized bat, which I guessed would have cost eight hundred dollars retail. Unfortunately, the bat was about three pounds four ounces and too heavy for me to wield with confidence, but it stayed in my cricket kit regardless—as with most things, more for the social capital than anything else.

The second bat—my first choice—was the Kookaburra Kahuna. The same bat that Ricky Ponting used to thrilling effect during his heyday, I was averaging 11.34 with in lower-grade cricket. The black tape at the bottom of the handle had worn away revealing a tightly bound white string underneath. I picked it up and twisted the handle around in my hands, studying the contours as if I were a marksman inspecting my rifle.

'Good pick up,' I whispered to myself involuntarily.

A full-length mirror had recently been mounted on the wall at the end of the room. I walked over and took my batting stance in front of it. I looked good as I stood there on the balls of my bare feet, squaring up to the invisible bowler.

Without even thinking, I nudged one off my hip behind square.

'Double up,' I whispered, tiptoeing from one end of the room and back, hyperconscious of the creaky floorboards.

I returned to in front of the mirror and took guard again. A picture of concentration, I allowed a delivery to go through to the keeper, scraping guard with my foot. The next ball shaped away and did me for bounce.

'Well bowled,' I mumbled under my breath to the imaginary bowler.

I took guard again and refocused, gently tapping the Kahuna on the wooden floor. This went on for about ten or fifteen minutes as I worked hard to get my eye in early. After a while, a few loose deliveries presented themselves and I was able to cash in and get my innings underway.

I was perspiring slightly at this point. I remembered that I used to stash a sweatband in the side pocket of my kit. I reached in and put it on, quietly admiring how it hid my discernibly receding hairline. Taking advantage of the mini-break, I allowed myself a sip of water from a glass on my desk. I didn't usually bat long enough to get to the drinks break.

I'd lost track of time—I was on about 30-odd by now. But just as I was mid-trigger movement for the next ball,

I saw the doorknob twist, slowly, in the reflection of the mirror. Frozen to the floor, there was nowhere to hide. I closed my eyes and waited for the inevitable.

It was Dad.

He stood in the doorway, silent, eyes wide open in a mixture of shock and bemusement. I vainly covered my modesty with the Kahuna—an ironic moment if ever there was one. I willed him to say something—anything—to break this painful silence. *You're not my real son. I'm disinheriting you.* Anything. As far as humiliations went, this was a new one. I'd heard horrifying stories about friends being caught 'pleasuring themselves' in their teenage years, the era of self-discovery. But being caught shadow batting in your bedroom at the age of thirty-one, completely naked (save for your cricket kit), must be up there. There is simply no explanation for that. At least masturbation has a tangible purpose, an outcome.

It took at least thirty seconds for him to compose himself, as if weighing up the best, most cutting comment to make—and he could have chosen from hundreds—before speaking.

'Dinner's ready,' he said in a soft, deep voice, before backing out of the room and closing the door gently.

5

FATHER AND SON MATCH

One of the things I discovered I missed most about playing cricket was the stories. Not the cricket so much, but the stories. The *banter*, if you'll excuse me using that tired fucking term that Australian and English men are so fond of (it goes without saying that the rate at which a bloke uses the word 'banter' is inversely proportional to the number of times he actually takes part in a witty exchange). Every good cricket team has a premier storyteller, a genuine raconteur who can tell a ripping yarn and leave the other ten blokes in hysterics.

And for much of my grade cricket career, that person was Bretty.

Last time I'd seen Bretty he was about to head off for yet another English summer. The usual informal arrangement with a mediocre village team: flight and accommodation sorted, a pound a run, substantial bar tab subsidy included. It's funny how the deals haven't evolved over the years, but to be fair, neither have the blokes. I'd asked a couple of my old cricket mates whether he was still over there, still tearing up the UK circuit with the fearsome intensity of a thousand suns, but no one knew where he was or what he was doing. He could easily have been dead, perhaps having pushed things a little too hard after a match-winning 30 not out.

I'd received a strange text out of the blue from an unknown number, but the language was spookily familiar.

Hey, champ. These still your digits? Just got back from the UK a few months ago. Beers?

Since this message could theoretically have come from seventy-five different people, I asked the question.

Sorry, who is this?

Haha. Mate, it's the Chop King!

I'd arranged to meet Bretty at his 'new digs' (his words, not mine). The suburb surprised me—he appeared to be residing in an exclusive, high-income postcode. I assumed he was either housesitting for a more successful mate or staying at a five-star rehab facility, so I didn't give it too much more thought. I walked up the long battleaxe driveway and pressed the doorbell.

'Championship!' he bellowed, pulling me into his chest for a bear hug, as if I'd just taken the key wicket in a second-grade semifinal.

'G'day, Bretty!'

'Come in, mate, make yourself at home.' He motioned towards the leather couch.

I hadn't seen Bretty for a good eighteen months, but he hadn't aged a day. That thick thatch of hair, the impressive bicep circumference, that famous twinkle in his eyes—a lively glint that said, 'Fuck it, I'm up for *anything*.' He was wearing a Mossimo singlet and white underpants (no pants), a look that for most people would immediately scream 'remote coastal town rapist', but somehow managed to work well on him. All the things that made him such a loveable character, and the lifeblood of any grade cricket team, were thankfully still on show.

Bretty hasn't changed! The world is as it should be!

'Want a beer?'

It was 10.30 a.m. on a Saturday, but I did want a beer. Bretty sensed it, smiled that winning smile, and in one fluid movement produced two glistening Heinekens from the fridge, cracking them open on his magnetic fridge bottle opener, then leaping athletically onto the couch.

He's still got it.

'Here's cheers!' We chinked glasses.

Last time I'd seen Bretty he was busily destroying the marriage of a lovely British lady in her late thirties. She had four young boys and lived in a beautiful house in the eastern suburbs with her workaholic investment banker husband, whom Bretty had memorably described as a 'cuck'. Bretty's inability to hold down full-time work had its advantages in that he was able to initiate countless sexual affairs with bored, neglected housewives. His inability to feel remorse was also highly advantageous. Bretty was a true pleasure seeker in every sense of the term, and no one wanted to settle down with a bloke who had no assets or career prospects, so it worked out well for all parties involved. Truth be told, I couldn't wait to hear what the Chop King had been up to over the past year or so. He used to sleep with roughly twenty women per season back in the day, so I figured he'd probably have added another forty or so by now, even if he was having a lean time of it.

'So, mate, any good circuit stories to share?'

A mischievous grin lit up his face. Just as he was about to answer, a black Range Rover swung into the driveway and out hopped four boys and a slim, dark-haired woman positively dripping in Prada. Half her face was covered by enormous bug-eyed sunglasses that seemed tinted to match the Range Rover windows. She power-walked towards the door as the children tumbled along ahead of her, a quartet of dark-featured scruffiness. I turned back to Bretty as she fumbled with the house keys.

'Mate, is that . . .'

'Yeah, that's Simone,' Bretty said. 'We got hitched two months back.'

In swept Simone and the boys.

'Darl, do you remember this bloke?' Bretty called, thumbing crudely towards me.

'Ah, of *course*! Hello, lovely, how *are* you?' Simone exclaimed, heaving the groceries onto the counter and prancing over, her high heels click-clacking on the marble floor—*click-clack, clickity-clack*—to proffer a pretentious European-style two-kiss greeting.

'I'm good, thanks. Wow, congratulations!' I managed, still mentally computing the fact that Bretty—the former

Chop King of our cricket club—was presumably now the legal stepfather to four young boys.

Simone glanced at her wedding ring and smiled.

'*Thanks*, hun. Bretty's been an absolute *rock* for me and the kids. I've never met such a wonderful, *caring* man.'

Hang on, is this the same bloke? Was I losing it? The same Bretty who used to boast openly about passing his symptomless chlamydia on to dozens of unsuspecting females?

'I know he used to be a bit of a *party animal* back in the day, but he's changed. Bretty's a dedicated stepfather to Rory, Hamish, Angus and Jaxon—he loves these kids like they're his own.'

Bretty nodded sheepishly before looking at his feet. 'Yeah, mate. No more circuits for me.'

A couple of moments passed to allow this shocking statement to sink in. *No more circuits?* Simone flashed a brief, eye-wateringly bright smile and shifted her eyes to the living room.

'Okay, boys, go upstairs and get changed for lunch!'

'Okay, Mum!'

The kids bounded upstairs together, their little footsteps almost in perfect sync.

'*Sooo*, has Bretty asked you yet?'

I was confused. 'Asked me what?'

Simone smiled.

'Well, we've got a wedding next weekend up in Brissy, but Jaxon, our eleven-year-old, has his father and son cricket match on. We can't miss the wedding, but *Jaxy* needs someone to go as his dad.'

'Yeah, that's right,' Bretty interjected. 'I don't suppose there's any chance you could step in for me, mate?'

'What, play on the fathers' team?'

'Yeah, that's right. It's just 20 overs a side—Fathers XI vs the Sons XI. Don't go too hard on them!' he joked, adding a wink as punctuation.

It was the first formal invitation I'd had to play cricket since that fateful day. Perhaps it was a sign? I'd just be doing Bretty a solid here, nothing more.

What harm can it do?

'Sure. What time should I pick him up?'

Ross McGrath was the self-appointed skipper for the Fathers XI. The founder and CEO of a tier-two telecommunications company servicing the corporate and government markets, Ross was just one of several high-flying businessmen on our team. This was a *private* school, after all, and I was playing alongside captains of industry—CEOs, CFOs, COOs—all on $250k-plus, at the very least. I was one of just three players not currently serving on a company board. I made a mental note to take advantage of these networking opportunities during the lunch break.

The Sons XI won the toss and had elected to bat. It was a beautiful morning—low twenties, a gentle south-easterly breeze blowing across the field. On so many occasions throughout my fledgling grade cricket career I'd stepped out onto the field on a brutal 43-degree day, wishing I was somewhere else, but today, in these beautiful surrounds, and without the self-imposed pressure of personal expectation, I found myself enjoying the serenity. The match was being played at the school itself, located in a leafy, affluent suburb, the ground lined by enormous trees. There was very little noise, save for the chirping of nearby birds and the scattered encouragement of middle-aged fathers to one another in the field. I half-expected a car full of fuckwits to hoon past and break the silence with a perfectly timed 'HOWZAT'— or perhaps an even cruder 'CRICKET'S SHIT'—but here I was, miles from the nearest grade cricket ground, in an area ranked among the state's highest for relative socio-economic advantages, according to the Australian Bureau of Statistics' five-yearly census of population and housing.

The match was humming along nicely. The kids were a few wickets down now, having earlier cashed in on one particularly poor spell of bowling by Milton Hendricks, a senior counsel who specialised in a variety of different areas of law, most notably intellectual property and consumer protection. Despite his extensive commercial experience and involvement in some of Australia's most prominent IP cases in recent years, Milton Hendricks was fucking useless with ball in hand. I could barely contain my laughter as Timmy Ashcroft—eleven-year-old son of Michael 'Mick' Ashcroft, a senior investment banker at one of Australia's 'Big Four'— peeled five straight boundaries off him. It beggared belief that someone could be so professionally distinguished yet lack any sort of physical coordination whatsoever.

I hadn't had to do much until Timmy pushed one into the vacant cover region, calling his batting partner, Tyson, through for a quick single. Struck by force of habit, I sprang off my toes and took a perfect line towards the ball, scooping it up with one hand and throwing down the metal stumps at the bowler's end in one slick motion. An audible 'whoa' reverberated around the ground; Timmy was out by five or six yards. Or so I thought. The team's coach, an athletically built PE teacher and former first grade cricketer, was officiating at square leg—and he had other ideas.

'Not out,' he called.

'GET FUCKED!' I yelled, involuntarily.

'No, he was just home,' the PE teacher hit back. The smug look on his face did not go unnoticed. 'And mind the language—there's kids around, *champ*.'

Inside me there was a not-insignificant part that wanted to take this further.

Not today, mate. This is for the kids. Remember, this is their day—not yours.

Perhaps sensing the potential for the situation to escalate, Ross McGrath called out for me to warm up.

'Next over that end, tiger,' he shouted, rolling both his arms energetically, as if he was competing in the hundred-metre butterfly.

The over ended and I handed my cap to the PE teacher. I measured out my run-up—six steps back and two across— and stood at the top of my mark. This was the first time I'd bowled since *that* match—*that fucking match*—where Nuggsy's indecent proposal had led to my immediate retirement from grade cricket. I blocked out the vision of Nuggsy feeding the spoils of the deceit into his preferred pokie machine, Cleopatra, and came in for my first delivery, a generously flighted full toss. Timmy stepped forward and drove it straight to cover, where his investment banker father, Mick, dropped an absolute sitter. It was obvious that he'd grassed it deliberately, judging by the histrionics.

'Sorry, champion! Too much heat on that one—did well to get a hand on it!' he called over from cover.

I smiled sarcastically and returned to my mark for my second delivery. This one slipped down leg, allowing Timmy to swivel on his heels and punish it for four.

'Wow, great shot! Cash in on the loose stuff, son!' Mick called from cover. He was really taking the piss now.

Timmy worked my next delivery in front of square for a single. As he ran through the crease, he came up to me, beaming.

'Excuse me, sir,' he asked politely.

'Yes, son?'

'Have you ever played cricket before?'

The fucking nerve of this kid!

Timmy's single had brought his batting partner on strike, some nameless kid. I lobbed up another loopy off spinner to him and he dollied it back to me. I sheepishly accepted the catch. The mid-wicket congregation was different— there was no 'yiewing' to mark the dismissal, nor was there an aggressive send-off for the young batsman. He'd played a terrible shot and had paid the ultimate price. In grade cricket his shot would have been met with mock laughter— it was unheard of to burgle a cheap wicket and not humiliate the batsman straight afterwards. But these were kids, after all, and we were adults. Fathers, even. We knew better than to do that.

My wicket brought Jaxy to the crease. At first glance

he appeared a highly organised young cricketer. He was wearing his thigh pad on the inside, for a start, which endeared him to me greatly. Most kids under the age of twelve wear their thigh pads on the outside, which always causes me a certain amount of anguish whenever I happen to come across a juniors' net session. Even though Jaxy was not Bretty's biological son, he still reminded me a lot of him. Not just the hairline—enviably steadfast, even for an eleven-year-old child yet to go through puberty—but his batting stance, in particular, was vintage Brett Smith. In I came for my first delivery to Jaxy, a drifting off spinner with a hint of overspin, only to watch him dance down the wicket and clip me elegantly wide of mid-on. He scurried down the pitch and slid his bat into the crease before turning back for the second run, easily making his ground. A strange familial pride overwhelmed me.

Shit, Jaxy can play. My son can play!

My next ball was faster, delivered at a lower trajectory, but Jaxy was into position early. With all the time in the world, he leaned back and played a deft late cut past first slip, which sped along the freshly manicured grass and all the way to the boundary. A burst of hearty applause rang out from the pavilion, mostly from the mothers who'd come along to support this good-natured family occasion.

I was trying to establish some eye contact with Jaxy, trying to suss him out, but he was resolutely focused, determined. In truth, I was reminded of the way I used to bat—back before years of harsh personal sledging had stolen my innocence and left me emotionally bruised, unable to clear my mind and focus on hitting runs. I was impressed, but also a little embarrassed that my 'son' was taking care of business with such clinical precision.

'Your kid can play, can't he?' McGrath yelled over from slip.

I instantly flashed back to my own Fathers vs Sons match in my final year of primary school. I was the school's star batsman, a dashing player of promise with the cricketing world at my feet. I arrived to the crease just as Dad had come into the attack. Having faced him thousands of times both in the nets and in the backyard, I knew Dad's bowling inside and out. At the same time, I knew that should I lose my wicket to him, he'd never let me live it down.

Dad had brought three men—literal *men*, adults ranging in age from mid-thirties to mid-fifties—in around the bat, creating Hitchcockian-like suspense, before casually ambling in to produce one of the most stunning deliveries I've ever faced to this day: a devastating off cutter that pitched on a good length and violently jagged back to clip my off bail. This was my equivalent of the Gatting Ball in the 1993 Ashes series, and Dad was Warney, lapping up his victory with oafish glee. In my defence, it was the first off cutter I had ever faced in my young life, since, generally speaking, eleven-year-old seam bowlers are yet to develop their wrists and fingers to the extent that they can successfully impart sideways movement. Some of the other fathers suggested I be given a reprieve for getting out first ball, but Dad wasn't having any of it. In retrospect, it was probably a bit over the top for him to point aggressively towards the pavilion and order me to 'fuck off, cunt', but he'd been made redundant earlier that week, so I can't hold it against him for wanting to blow off a bit of steam.

To make things worse, Dad still brings this story up every Christmas without fail, exaggerating certain details around the delivery and its general unplayability. Later that match, Dad proceeded to smack my pre-teen teammates to all parts of the ground on his way to an unbeaten 50-odd. Lofted drives, full-blooded pulls, each six bigger than the last. To make things worse, he had a habit of shouting 'shit ball' whenever he punished a particularly yuck delivery (a technique he'd picked up during our regular net sessions, which he claimed was all about encouraging me to bowl better). Our opening bowler, Nicholas Thornton, ran to the pavilion in tears after Dad's third consecutive six, a towering maximum that seemed to hang in the air for months, eventually settled on the roof of the PE centre. The shot was accompanied by a maniacal laugh that echoed around the otherwise silent ground. Like so many kids that day, that was to be Nicholas's last season of cricket.

I vowed to myself that I would be a gracious surrogate parent to Jaxon. Yes, I was a former grade cricketer—and I'd wear that unfortunate tag until the day I died—but those days were over now, and I refused to be defined by my past. I'd grown a lot, emotionally speaking, since my final match of grade. In that eighteen-month period, I'd managed to successfully reassimilate into normal society. I had a full-time job. A girlfriend. A two-bedroom apartment seven kilometres from the city centre. Yes, I had recently lost all of those things, but still, the fact that I had been able to accumulate them at some point surely meant something in terms of my personal development, didn't it? This was my opportunity to break the cycle of generational dysfunction. No, I would not obliterate Jaxy's self-esteem for my own selfish kicks, as Dad had done to me. I completed my over without incident and patted Jaxy on the back and told him to 'go on with it'. I watched with great pride as he went on to retire on 30 not out, helping to steer the Sons XI to a formidable total of 112 off their allotted 20 overs.

After all, this day wasn't about me; it was about little Jaxy. Or some shit.

We crept along at two runs an over for the first five or six overs, as unathletic middle-aged men struggled to navigate prepubescent, sub-seventy-k-an-hour bowling on astro. These titans of business were no match for their own offspring. They may have conquered the corporate world but their techniques were decidedly yuck. Furthermore, it wasn't like they were being done all ends up by good bowling. Blokes were throwing their wickets away, hitting long hops to mid-wicket, missing straight ones. For a split second I wondered whether Nuggsy had fixed this match too. Did his insidious tentacles spread their way down to under-12 school cricket?

I was set to come in at eight—a position I was familiar with, especially towards the back end of my grade career— and had not expected to bat, but a rush of wickets brought me to the crease in the ninth over. Still eleven overs to go. It wasn't even 11 a.m. yet.

Just poke a few around, don't get carried away.

Their off spinner came in for his third over. He must have weighed 30 kilos tops; his matchstick frame was exaggerated by a comically large head, which bobbled from side to side as he stammered towards the crease. The ball left his hand and sailed towards me gently. I could have done sixteen sudoku puzzles in the time it took to reach me. I put one big adult foot forward and prodded it back down the wicket to a chorus of young, encouraging voices.

'Well bowled, Jackson!'

Fuck me, is every kid these days called Jackson? Does he spell his name with an 'x' as well?

I took a single off the last ball of the over and went down the wicket to have the obligatory conversation with my batting partner, a 35-year-old bloke by the name of Phil. I felt I knew Phil from somewhere, but I couldn't quite place him. He had a lean build, wispy moustache and a hint of a rat's tail, which sat at odds with the clean short-back-and-sides appearance of our bloated C-suite teammates. During the warm-up, I'd noticed that Phil had a bit more skill than the other men. I think it was the way he bent down and threw the ball at the stump in one smooth motion, a level of coordination that implied he'd done this sort of thing before at a decent level. Anyway, Phil was sitting pretty on about 24 not out, holding the innings together.

'Which of these kids is yours?' I asked.

'I'm actually filling in for my brother. My nephew is the little bloke at deep mid-wicket,' he answered, pointing towards another rake-thin kid on the boundary.

'Ah, okay. I'm filling in for a mate as well.'

'I actually used to play a bit of grade back in the day. You look familiar—did you used to play?'

I froze momentarily.

'Yeah, I did, actually. Mostly in second and third grade.'

'Ah, that's where I know you from. I think I remember playing against you out at Hislop #2 and one of your quicks—some bald bloke—called me a "fucking paedophile". I'll never forget it.'

'Yeah, that was one of Nuggsy's go-to sledges.'

'Fuck, he was a real cunt, wasn't he?'

Reflexively, I went to reply with *he's actually a really good bloke if you get to know him*, but then thought better of it in light of recent events.

'Yeah, he *is* a cunt.'

'Is he still playing?' Phil asked.

'Actually, I haven't seen him in a while.'

'I heard he was involved in some kind of match-fixing stuff. You hear anything about that?'

My heart skipped a beat.

'What'd you hear?'

'Oh, just rumours—nothing specific . . .'

We bumped gloves and returned to our respective ends for the start of the new over. But Phil's comment about match-fixing had sparked something in me. Even though this was just a bit of hit and giggle for the kids, I didn't want it to descend into farce.

Timmy Ashcroft had been thrown the ball. In the car ride on the way to the ground, Jaxy told me that Timmy had been bullying him over a period of two years. Timmy was big for his age—tall and well-built, muscular even, especially for an eleven-year-old, the beneficiary of early onset puberty—and had a clear physical advantage over his teammates. Timmy's first ball was a good twenty k's faster than the previous kid's. Even though that made the delivery just ninety kilometres an hour tops, I was nonetheless startled by the extra pace. It shaped away in the air and continued off the seam, forcing me to play and miss in an ungainly fashion.

'You're kidding me,' Timmy remarked in a high-pitched voice as he followed through to a standstill.

Hang on, this kid is sledging me?

A couple of his young teammates clapped approvingly, although by the lack of intensity it was clear that he was an unpopular figure among the Sons XI, much as his father, Mick, was proving among the Fathers XI. During the innings change, Mick had entertained his fellow fathers with an unsolicited sexual tale involving his 24-year-old secretary, a transparent attempt to cement his status as the team's official Chop King. Every cricket team has a Chop King, and the Fathers XI was proving no different. Mick had little competition in this regard, especially with Bretty absent from the fold; after all, the rest of the team were mostly mild-mannered businessmen between the ages of thirty-five and fifty, all happily married with a couple of young children and residing in safe Liberal seats, living a comfortable existence on a combined household income of $400,000-plus. Put simply, they weren't 'smashing birds' on the weekends. What was clear, though, was that this bloke was a fucking *flog*—and that the apple didn't fall far from the tree.

I could hear Mick cheering in the distance.

'Come on, Timmy. Dig one in. *Lid* the bastard!'

I looked over to Jaxy at mid-wicket, standing there in his short cricket shorts, all thirty kilograms of him. Growing up, Dad always said that the best way to learn things was the hard way. It was for this reason that at the age of twelve he had me doing his tax returns for my 'own good'. It seemed strange at the time, but on the upside, I was the first twelve-year-old at my school to have advanced proficiency in Microsoft Excel. Maybe it fell upon me to teach Timmy a hard lesson now, before he reached adulthood and became just another fuckwit grade cricketer, sledging teenagers for sport in order to fill a gaping emotional void.

Timmy's delivery was full and straight, perfectly in my arc. In one fluid motion, I leaned into the shot and extended my arms fully. The ball pinged off the blade so sweetly that I could barely feel the impact. We all marvelled as it thudded against the third-floor balcony of the school's science building, before rebounding back onto the field and arriving at a standstill just metres from Jaxy at mid-wicket.

Six runs.

'You've just bombed my kid!' Mick shouted from the boundary.

I looked around to see him shaking his fist in anger. A few of the other men had half-heartedly congregated around him, but I could tell from their body language that they were quietly pleased. Undoubtedly, their own sons had informed them of Timmy's bully behaviour. They'd probably been dreaming of doing the same thing today, but lacked the cricketing ability to pull it off. It was up to me—the former grade cricketer—to teach Timmy this long-overdue lesson in respect. Truth be told, the shot was as much for them as it was for me. It was the first time in weeks that I'd felt 'something'. God, it was wonderfully intoxicating.

Maybe I still had a bit of cricket left in me, after all?

The kid ran in again and dished up another full straight one with zero revolutions on it. And again, and again. Once I'd started, I couldn't stop. I was relishing the opportunity to feel bat on ball. It didn't matter where Timmy landed it, because I was in the zone. I raised my bat to the pavilion as I departed the field, retired not out on 31 (off nine balls). We eventually fell short in our run chase, providing the Sons XI with a feel-good moment that they would remember forever. Timmy had learned a valuable lesson today as well: if you're going to sledge me, make sure you fucking back it up with some heat.

As I drove Jaxy home, chatting about the game, the sound of ABC *Grandstand* humming on the stereo, I briefly entertained the thought of signing up for a coaching accreditation course. Yes, I could be the one to steer these kids on the right track. Just as Lara was helping educate kids in Central America, I would be the one to educate the young cricketers of Australia. Someone needed to get to them early, before they were trapped in the spiralling vortex of desperation that is grade cricket. Maybe *I* could be that 'someone'.

I'd slammed the door shut on cricket eighteen months ago, but it appeared that door was now slightly ajar.

I slung my kit down on the porch and fumbled for my house keys. Normally there would be a few lights on, a television buzzing in the background, but the family house was eerily quiet as I stepped inside. I longed for the sound of cricket on TV, the true sound of summer—the coarseness of Taylor, Warne, Healy and co; the smooth, dulcet tones of the debonair Englishman Mark Nicholas—but that was not to be, as Dad had recently disconnected the television in an effort to get me out of the house as much as possible. Not for the first time, I pondered how on earth Mark Nicholas had managed to score such a sweet gig in the dog-eat-dog world of Australian sports broadcasting when he hadn't even played test cricket for *his* country (let alone the country whose TV cricket coverage he was anchoring). Seriously, give a mediocre cricketer a good tan and a bouffant 'salad' and watch him soar.

'In here, son,' a voice called out from the dining room.

I followed the sound, fumbling my way through the darkness, to find Mum and Dad seated at the dinner table, lights still off. A carafe of wine sat in the middle of the table, half-finished. The table was set, but there was no food to be seen.

'Where's the grub?' I asked. 'We ordering fish and chips tonight?'

I couldn't make out her face in the darkened room, but I could tell by the rapid up-and-down movement of her shoulders that Mum was sobbing silently.

Dad cleared his throat and took control of the situation.

'Mate, look. It's just not working out.'

I exhaled slowly. Yes, the timing was a surprise, but the

outcome was hardly unexpected. I just wondered why it had taken so long for them to make the decision. I thought back to high school and all the muffled arguments I over-heard late at night. The times that Mum would break down in tears for no reason whatsoever. Secretly, I'd envied children of divorce. They were always a bit cooler; a bit worldlier. Finn, my best non-cricket mate, had his parents go through a divorce back when he was in Year 7. It was a real shock at the time, especially when his mum quickly remarried an Italian bloke in his late thirties. Matteo, an artist in his native Florence, had introduced Finn to visual arts, music, food and culture, helping to shape him into the fine young man he is today. Meanwhile, my dad was intro-ducing me to the short ball off sixteen yards in the nets after a tough day at work.

'Sorry to hear that, Dad. I know that divorce can be difficult. But fifty per cent of marriages these days end in—'

'What are you talking about? Your mother and I are fine!'

'Y . . . you're not getting a divorce?'

'Fuck no. *You're* moving out.'

'What?'

'Yep, you've got to move out. *Pack 'em*. It's not working, champ.'

I looked over to the corner of the room. My bags sat there together in a neat little bundle. Pack 'em indeed.

'Hang on, what are you talking about? I've got nowhere else to go,' I tried.

'I saw you leave this morning with your cricket kit. You've been playing cricket again, haven't you?'

The way he'd phrased that last sentence made it sound like I'd suffered a heroin relapse. Now, just to be clear, I've never done heroin in my life. *Cricket* was my drug of choice (although I don't mind a bag every now and then, I must admit, as long as someone else is paying). Not to underplay the devastating effects of heroin or anything, but in my experience, cricket is the most insidious drug of all. I've talked already about the sweet, ephemeral pleasure of a perfectly timed cover drive, but it's the comedown that's the hardest. Once it takes hold of you, it's very hard to get 'off' cricket.

For years, I tried unsuccessfully to wean myself off the game, but it never worked. Nuggsy's match-fixing offer was the final straw, the catalyst I needed to go cold turkey (which is the only way you can get off cricket—you have to just stop playing, change your phone number, run in the opposite direction and never look back). But now, eighteen months sober, I'd allowed myself to forget how low things had gotten towards the end. Meanwhile, Dad had seen all the red flags come up again. For starters, he'd walked in on me shadow batting naked—probably the first clear sign that a relapse was imminent. He'd seen me squinting at the grade cricket results in the back of the broadsheet paper, which indicated a reinvigorated interest in the competition. And now, there was circumstantial evidence to suggest that I had participated in a cricket match today.

'Yes, of course you have,' Dad continued, taking my silence as an admission. 'So why don't you go and stay with one of your mates? Or whatever. But you're not staying here, coasting off us, wasting your time playing cricket. You know what it did to Nuggsy.'

'What do you mean about Nuggsy?' I blurted, fearful that news of the match-fixing scandal had made its way to Dad. Christ, the mere thought gave me chills.

'The bloke is a no-hoper. All those cricket blokes are. If you're still playing cricket into your thirties, you've got to ask yourself some serious life questions.'

Fuck, Dad isn't holding back here.

'Listen, son,' he continued, his tone now softening. 'You've got a chance at making something of yourself—so go on, get out of here and get *on* with it. Uni, a career, all of it. Staying here won't do you any good.'

Clearly, there was no reasoning with Dad on this topic. I wanted to tell him I was only helping out Bretty in a Fathers vs Sons game—a game I'd greatly enjoyed—but deep down I knew Dad didn't give a shit about what kind of cricket it was. In his eyes, cricket was cricket. Grade, Shires, park or school—whatever the level, it was all bad. My stay in the house came with a single yet unspoken rule: you can live here, as long as you're not playing cricket. In Dad's eyes, my decision to play for the Fathers XI constituted a breach of contract, thus triggering the immediate termination of our agreement. But even deeper down, right in the very core of my being, I knew that cricket had an inexorable hold on me. It was clear that the more I tried to resist, the more it beckoned; indeed, a gravitational force was pulling me towards the game once more. Why fight this Stockholm syndrome any longer?

I had to leave, and that was that.

I walked over to the bags, slung them up onto my shoulder and made my way towards the front door. Mum swivelled around in her chair. At that angle, the streetlight hit her face, and I could see that her wide eyes were full to the brim with tears.

'Where are you going to go, love?' she asked, her voice breaking with emotion.

There was only one place left for me to go.

6

LIVING SOMEWHERE ELSE NOW

I trudged up the cobblestoned path, head bowed suffi- ciently to take in the overgrown weeds that lined the edges. Light rain fell and I looked up to glimpse a sheet of lightning above. Reflexively, I hoped for a crack of thunder to follow—usually you'd be off the field if it came within thirty seconds. That crack would be the indicator for rain. Rain that alleviated the anxiety that preceded failure. Big, beautiful rain. But I didn't play cricket anymore, so all of these thoughts were merely bad habits.

I'd brought with me what I had, my worldly possessions contained in one bag—my cricket kit, obviously. I stood and faced the weathered door, lost, dazed, lonely, seeking refuge. This was a door I'd faced many times, though never in this circumstance. I released the kit from my tense grasp. It fell to the concrete with the dull thud that only a kit can conjure. I squared up to the door, took a breath and rapped it with my knuckle three times. Always three. A moment passed, then heavy footsteps. I wondered whether I'd taken too big a gamble coming here.

The door swung open. There was silence, followed by an embrace. A real, genuine embrace.

'I missed you, mate,' said the hulking man in front of me.

He wrapped his giant arms around me, exemplifying dignified physical emotion. Thunder cracked above.

'Missed you too, Nuggsy. Mate, I'm struggling here. Lara's left me. Mum and Dad have kicked me out. I didn't know where else to go.'

'Don't worry about that. You'll stay here.'

At this he let me go. 'Come on, mate, get inside. It's about to bucket down. Hear that thunder? Days gone by we'd be straight off and into the cans for sure . . .'

Nuggsy immediately stiffened upon completing the sentence, as though remembering that perhaps we weren't at full-scale mates level quite yet. Everything about both his body language and verbal language had screamed elation at my arrival, but he didn't want to ruin it. While I was the one with the immediate problem, I couldn't help but view him with some joy: a man desperately happy at the return of his scorned friend, yet trying vainly to contain the inherent vulnerability that would come by conveying that happiness. Right on cue, he compensated.

'Anyway, what the fuck's happened, mate? You've not played up, have you?' he asked with a smirk, deftly repositioning himself into a power position within the conversation.

'No, no. Nothing like that at all, mate.'

The lump in my throat grew as I briefly reconnected with the scene back at Lara's, then Mum and Dad's. As I searched for the words, Nuggsy twigged that this was a case of a broken heart. He let me off the hook.

'You know what, mate? Don't worry about it. You look pretty fucking cut up. Sit down. Want a beer?'

Yes. I wanted a beer.

We sat at Nuggsy's table—and it was *his* table—and briskly caught up about the last eighteen months, the way blokes are able to do over a solitary beer. In these conversations, men will without irony reduce descriptions of their life to 'not much, mate'. Sometimes, such a description might be accurate; at least, I think it may have been true of Nuggsy. He was labouring—literally, and figuratively, I suppose—and circuiting too. His rig was somehow still in enviably colossal order. He was scraping by financially, and his eyes lit up when he told of a recent win on the pokies. Nothing had really changed, aside from the house itself. I'd been here before, but an entirely new iteration of housemates was now in place. This was important information as I hadn't been sure whether Nuggsy's spontaneous embrace and kind words amounted to little. Did 'you'll stay here' mean a couple of days? Nuggsy went on to say that someone had recently left. She was apparently a gorgeous, 'very organised' woman, who sadly had to move out of the house at short notice. Her swift departure left me wondering whether Nuggsy had been sexually inappropriate towards her. But also, more selfishly, whether this may have opened up a more permanent vacancy for myself.

'But back to you. What are your plans?'

Nuggsy's feet were raised on the table as he rocked back in his chair, now lighting a smoke, beer close by. You really couldn't overstate his delight, however cool he tried to play it. He seemed to be relishing the fact I needed something from him.

'I don't know, mate. I'm at a loss. I came straight here after it happened. I don't know. I just . . . don't know.'

'Well, where are you going to live, great man?' said Nuggsy, still reclining, like Gordon Gekko toying with a lowly Wall Street pawn.

'I . . . I have no idea, Nuggsy. I mean . . .'

I fumbled for words as I tried to summon the courage to simply ask him what we both knew I wanted to ask. Alas, I was also a man, which naturally meant I had to avoid asking for help at all costs. Nuggsy wasn't making it easy.

'I see you've brought your kit. I know you're not planning on playing again, so I'm guessing your threads are in there?'

He zeroed his gaze on me comically, drawing this excruciating exchange out as long as he could. I couldn't take it much longer.

'Look, Nuggsy,' I said, a little more straightforward now. 'I've just broken up with my long-term partner. Not only have I lost someone I cared about, I've lost a place to live too. Would you consider having me stay at yours? If it's for a short time, I'd appreciate it. If it was something more permanent, I'd be over the moon. I don't want to impose, but if you have space you'd be recruiting a much-improved domestic figure. Since living with Lara I've developed an appreciation for and diligence in cooking, cleaning, washing dishes, vacuuming, landlord relations, and hedge-trimming. I know you could use me here. Will you have me?'

Nuggsy leaned back even further now, so much so that I worried the seat might come out from under him. Yet he radiated the look of a man who knew every inch of his domain, his palace. He took a long drag of his cigarette before exhaling three perfectly formed smoke rings, expertly building the tension as I waited for his verdict.

'Look, bud,' he eventually said, pausing to dispose of his cigarette before taking a lengthy swill of his beer. 'These deals are never easy. There's a lot to consider, and I'll have to speak to the house.'

'Speak to the house about what?' came a booming voice from down the hall.

I caught the silhouette of another absolute specimen coming towards me before realising it was my old mate Bruiser. He looked every inch the corporate type: slim-fitting suit, tie slightly undone to signal day's end, designer gym bag and the clunk of heavy heel on floorboards to denote a pricey shoe. I was stunned to see him, truth be known. Last time I saw Bruiser he was living in one of those prime areas that straddled urban and suburban, and well on the way to acquiring a second property to match his late-model Alfa Romeo. Now here he was, bellowing to Nuggsy, who himself was clothed in a dark blue singlet and black Puma tracksuit pants tucked into his socks. I suddenly noticed the fruit bowl on the table was full of cricket balls.

'Well, well, well,' Bruiser continued, now standing in the doorway. 'What brings you to our humble abode, Champions League?'

Bruiser and I had always had warm respect for each other. He was one of those guys—and it's rare in sport—where you don't have to second-guess him. I was genuinely happy to see him, even if he'd champed me on first sight.

'Bruiser, it's a pleasure, mate. The truth is I'm not here in the best circumstances, but I'm better for seeing you.' I eyed him up and down. 'What a marvellous rig you have, mate. Seriously.'

'Ah, that's too kind. I think the suit helps. Now, what's happening here? What's going on?'

The pleasantries were, well, pleasant, but Bruiser—a derivatives trader at a major multinational investment bank—needed outcomes. He knew how to get information and was habitually focused on progress. Word has it that he once delivered a SWOT analysis, P&L statement and ten points of recommendation at a selection meeting when he filled in as fourth grade captain. His snappy request for information was entirely in keeping with his character.

'In short, Bruiser—and I know you like it short—Lara and I have parted ways. I've come around to see Nuggsy and to enquire, I guess, about whether there might be a bed here. Nuggsy was just telling me that he'd have to discuss it with the house.'

'Nuggsy's talking shit, mate,' came Bruiser's reply. 'We'd love to have you. We've needed a solid presence in the house. Besides, a bird left last week, so we've got a spot to fill. It's done. You're in. Nuggsy, sort him out the room upstairs.'

'Well, fuck me!' Nuggsy boomed mockingly. 'The house CEO has spoken!'

Nuggsy and Bruiser had clearly not relented in their

near-decade quest for alpha dominance in their relationship. It really was something to behold. Two giant
roosters forever claiming physical, political, social, mental,
emotional and spiritual territory, which are the six key
pillars of alpha life.

Nuggsy looked at me now. 'Seriously, mate. I was fucking
with you. This is the best thing since that yoga *tunza* at The
Bridge—remember her?—used ropes that time. Really, this
is wonderful stuff. There was never any question, you're
with us now.'

Nuggsy punctuated the sentence with a throaty
'yiiiiiieeeewwwww!'. Bruiser joined in for the back half of
it, two grown men engaging in a modern-day animalistic
howl.

'But hang on. What about your other housemate? I really
don't want to impose.'

Nuggsy let out a contorted snort, while Bruiser just
laughed.

'Nath won't mind, mate,' Nuggsy scoffed. 'Trust me, he'll
do what we say.'

That worked for me. Nuggsy then let out a piercing
farmer's whistle, as though he was calling for a cattle dog at
least a kilometre away.

'Nath!' he bellowed. 'Get down here, pal. There's someone
we'd like you to meet.'

Nuggsy whistled again, though this time it was for show,
as we could already see Nath coming.

Sidling up to me was 23-year-old Nathan Evans, all
six-foot-one of him, blond, tanned, sinewy. His hair hung
long, curling ever so slightly as it fell over his ears and neck.

His casual black T-shirt was loose enough to suggest an interest in arts and culture, but tight enough to hint he knew the value of chest and biceps and incorporated a consistent, split routine in and around cricketing, university and work commitments. Nathan exuded a surfy calm that would have endeared him to sexual suitors, though I doubted it would play well in cricketing circles. His story already intrigued me.

'We've got someone, Nath,' Nuggsy announced. 'An old mate of Bruiser and mine. Played at our club too.'

At this point Nath looked awkwardly at Nuggsy, then Bruiser, then me.

'Is this, um, your mate?' asked Nath sheepishly.

'Yes, yes, Nath. Fuck, mate,' Nuggsy shooshed him. 'There's no need to spell it right out. This is him. Yes, we made a mistake. Yes, we've served our time. Yes, we're moving on with it. Starting with him literally moving in today.'

It's always strange when a conversation about you happens around you, so I intervened.

'Nath—or is it Nathan? Nice to meet you, mate.' I said, as genially as possible.

'Nice one, bud. Welcome.'

'Nathan,' I shot back. 'Please, for the love of God, do *not* call me "bud".'

'I . . . I'm sorry mate. It's just that they . . .'

Nathan gestured to Nuggsy and Bruiser, who both exploded with laughter. I was confused, and Nath looked unmoved either way.

'We've asked that Nath address any guest or new entrance

to the house—or "the fortress", as I call it—with the suffix "chief", "pal", "boss", "champ" or—in your case—"bud",' Bruiser explained. 'Your reaction didn't disappoint.'

'Sorry, mate,' Nath apologised. 'I really didn't want to.'

'Don't worry, Nath, I've been there,' I replied, sympathy welling for this kid so obviously already caught in the social crosshairs of grade cricket.

It crossed my mind that I might be able to share some wisdom with him one day—wisdom that I wish I'd been told when I was coming through the grades.

'Well, I hope you don't mind me staying here,' I volunteered to Nath.

'Not at all. It's fine,' he said. He had impressed me already.

'That's the spirit, chieftain!' I said, feeling jovial.

Cheers and guffaws followed from Bruiser, though by this stage Nuggsy had started walking down the hall. I was quick to let Nath know that I was only 'chiefing' him ironically, though these days I find it hard to tell the difference between irony and sincerity, not least within myself.

All of a sudden I heard a loud 'oi!'. I turned to Nuggsy, who was beckoning me to what I guessed was his room. It *must* have been his room, because there were three cricket bats outside the door. Nuggsy's rapid gesturing suggested I needed to get there quickly, so I hurried along. He shooed me in and closed the door behind him, like an adolescent keen on refuge from his parents.

I wasn't sure what to expect when entering Nuggsy's room, although I'd braced myself for pandemonium. I'd heard so many of his stories over the years but had never pictured anything like this.

'Shoes off, please,' Nuggsy commanded.

It was the neatest room occupied by a mid-thirties male that I had ever laid eyes on. Polished wooden floorboards gave way to carefully placed furniture, including the centrepiece of his room, a king-sized four-poster bed with six symmetrically placed pillows, the mattress covered by a designer quilt with silk edging. To face out from his bed was to be exposed to 180-degree views of the city, a remarkable feat given the rough, industrial setting this place was in. To face in to his bed was not so much surprising as jolting. On the wall at the head of the bed, directly above the pillows, was a life-sized poster of Mark Waugh. There he was in 1997, decked out in green Australian test helmet and Slazenger gear, casually clipping one off his legs in his inimitable style, overlooking the room like a Hindu deity. It was then that Nuggsy's stories came flooding back to me. He had always made a point of highlighting his love of sex in the missionary position. It occurred to me that this would expose him to Mark Waugh's gaze were he to briefly raise his head during sexual liaisons.

'Nuggsy, please don't tell me you look at Mark Waugh while you're having sex . . .'

Silence ensued, a lascivious smirk slowly creeping across his face.

'You really are sick, aren't you, mate?'

'They don't seem to mind, mate,' he grinned.

But back to the state of Nuggsy's room: I had never realised he was so clean. By contrast the shared living area was a disaster, dirty dishes with tiny pieces of Hokkien noodles still yet to be wiped and disposed of on every available surface. In the kitchen the sink was full of a browny-black soup reminiscent of soy sauce and coffee dregs, with a dank smell that suggested fresh air hadn't entered in some time. But Nuggsy's room offered heavenly respite, like stepping into the Shangri-la after time in downtown Mogadishu.

I turned to his wardrobe, admiring his arrangement of jackets, jumpers, vests and collared shirts, all hung seasonally. As my eyes scanned the blazer section, something hidden behind the hung clothes caught my eye. Curious, I slid Nuggsy's winter wear to one side to reveal a faded picture, attached to the wall with stickytape, of a stunning vineyard complete with luminescently green lush grass and an ancient wooden barrel bathed in sunshine. Squinting, I could just make out some words handwritten in faint cursive.

Alaîn, mon cheri. Ta maison, Amboise, Vallée de la Loire.

'Nugg, what's this?' I asked immediately.

Nuggsy had been recounting Mark Waugh's 116 in Port Elizabeth, but upon realising I was halfway into his closet, he charged over and, with uncharacteristic urgency, drew his clothes to cover the picture.

'It's nothing, champ,' he said. 'You don't need to get so deep into my stuff.'

I backed off straight away.

'Sorry, mate, don't mean to pry,' I apologised.

Perhaps it was time to address the other elephant in the room.

'Look, Nuggsy, about the fixing stuff . . .'

'Let's leave the past in the past,' he said, cutting me off. 'Look, mate,' he continued, 'I'm really glad you're here.

I think this can be a new start for you. Whatever's happened is done, and I reckon there's a good opportunity for you to build something here. The boys are good: Bruiser's always got his shit together, Nath's a good kid, I'm doing my thing, and you've come a long way yourself, by the looks of it. I think we can make a real fist of this. What do you say? Will you take the room upstairs for a couple of months at least? It's yours if you want it.'

I couldn't believe how fast everything was moving. In the space of a few weeks I'd gone from mulling proposals, the housing market and a future with Lara, to living with my parents, to being essentially homeless. This was a wild fucking narrative, indeed. Now, here I was, standing in Nuggsy's incongruously clean room, the newest member of a share house solely comprising grade cricketers. I hadn't had time to process anything. Even so, I was buoyed to have rekindled my friendship with Nuggsy, however silent the reconciliation was.

'Nuggsy, we've had our differences, and your room has scared me a little bit, but you're a great friend. I'm really grateful that you're willing to take me in on zero notice . . .'

Time to take ownership. Time to be a little selfish.

'I'd love to stay.'

7

CIRCUIT

The allure of the Saturday night circuit is, for many grade cricketers, the only reason they're still playing. They got over the cricket part of cricket long ago but stayed for the ritualistic binge drinking that ensued a day's play. Over the course of one's career, the circuit gradually begins to take higher precedence over scoring runs or taking wickets, until eventually your blood alcohol level on a Sunday morning exceeds your actual batting average.

Nuggsy, in particular, lived for Saturdays. These days he didn't care about the actual playing of the sport; he just loved to be around his cricket friends. During the week, Nuggsy's cricket friends all went back to their wives and girlfriends and jobs, but on Saturday he had them. Saturday was Nuggsy's day and night with the kids. Since my own retirement from grade cricket, such Saturday nights had typically been spent with Lara. We'd order takeaway and binge-watch some highly acclaimed television series on Netflix, before drifting off to sleep in each other's arms at around 11.30 p.m. Occasionally we would catch up with another couple for dinner at a restaurant, usually one strongly endorsed on *Broadsheet,* and indulge in a bottle of good wine and some intellectually stimulating conversation before ordering an Uber and heading back to Lara's apartment. Yes, I was living the cliché yuppie lifestyle, albeit on a gross salary of $45,000.

But tonight, I wasn't scrolling the UberEATS app with Lara, debating whether to order Thai or Italian. Tonight, I was standing in the kitchen with my new housemates—Nuggsy, Bruiser and Nathan—in a semicircle formation, clutching a beer like my life depended on it. The night was young—even if we were not—and full of possibilities. The semicircle formation in which we'd found ourselves was an unconscious decision, yet another unfortunate symptom of a lifetime of cricket. Team selections, stretching, slips practice, drinking—all of these activities are best executed in semicircle formation. I half-expected Nuggsy to pick a cricket ball out of the fruit bowl and start a fielding drill. *'Let's get ten, boys,'* he'd shout, with urgency. *'No one's leaving until we get ten catches in a row . . .'*

Instead, Nuggsy looked at my half-full beer and sneered.

'You nursing that, mate?'

I was indeed nursing it, but who in their right mind would admit to that?

'Nah, mate. Grab us another one, yeah?'

I've always said that you can tell a lot about a man by

the contents of his fridge. A neat, well-stacked fridge with plenty of fruit and vegetables, dairy products, meat and fish indicates an individual who is in control of his life—or, at the very least, has a basic understanding of nutrition, not to mention has the necessary funds for a week's worth of groceries. By contrast, Nuggsy had one of the sorriest-looking fridges I'd ever come across. The vegetable tray was completely empty and there was no milk to be seen. In fact, all that was there were four sixpacks of (admittedly premium) lager and several empty wheels of cheese. What's more, the sixpacks had fucking Post-it notes on them. The word 'Nuggler' had been scrawled on the notes in marker pen, a fair warning to anyone who dared to nab one of the precious lagers.

'Looks like you might want to get some shopping in, Nugget,' I joked.

'Don't need a fridge if you smash your takeaway on the first attempt, legend!'

Nuggsy plucked five beers from the fridge, handing one each to Bruiser, Nathan and me, leaving himself double-parked with a 'soldier' in each mitt. With rotelike ease, he opened one of his beers by grabbing the second bottle around the bottom of its neck and placing its cap under the edge of the other bottle's cap. He then used the second bottle for leverage to press down to release the cap of the first beer. I remembered the first time I'd seen Nuggsy do this trick, back in my first season as an impressionable nineteen-year-old. I'd immediately consulted YouTube to try to replicate it myself but only ended up getting into a heated argument with an anonymous stranger in the comments section about whether George Bush 'did' 9/11. With that done, Nuggsy then opened the second bottle with his teeth. I should probably point out that these bottles were twist tops. Yes, I could tell by this unnecessary display of alphadom—plus the fact that his eyes had glazed over—that Nuggsy had entered 'circuit mode'.

I looked over to see how the other lads were going. Bruiser was vigorously swiping away on his phone, which either meant he was on a dating app, ordering a bag, or searching properties on the realestate.com app. A text message lit up his phone, prompting a half-smile and a flurry of fingers. With Bruiser, I always wondered what was going on behind the phone. He scratched his enviably thick beard and took a hearty gulp of his premium lager. The beer bottle looked tiny in his enormous hands, just as the ball did when he was sending down his 125 kilometre per hour outswingers. Bruiser was a formidable physical presence. His brown R.M. Williams boots gave him an extra inch of height (which, at six-four, he did not need) and, more importantly, the impression that he spent the occasional long weekend on a rural property. What was more impressive, however, was his crisp white collared shirt, at least seven shades whiter than any set of cricket whites I'd seen in my lifetime. Bruiser's beard went down to the bottom of his neck, at which point the hair just stopped abruptly, as if under a new jurisdiction. Naturally, Bruiser had opted to undo the top four buttons, which had the added impact of exposing his sculpted chest. There was no doubt that Bruiser had his chest professionally waxed that very morning, but this was a new era of masculinity, where waxed chests were *de rigueur*.

Bruiser was an early adopter of chest waxing; indeed, his glistening chest had prompted dozens of players to embrace this waxing culture, so much so that Soo Lin's Waxing Parlour was named an official sponsor of the club, with the emblem now adorning the training jerseys.

Nathan, meanwhile, was holding firm in the semi-circle. I was slightly taken aback by his posture, which mirrored Nuggsy's to a tee. I could tell that Nuggsy and Nathan were on the exact same weights program. Despite having completely different body types, their proportions were now almost identical. I knew for a fact that Nuggsy didn't have a gym membership, but apparently Nathan— a platinum member at Fitness First—had been sneaking Nuggsy in and out of gyms around the state under the guise that Nuggsy was 'interested in checking out the facilities'. Like all of us, he was clutching his beer so tightly that small veins were popping out from his biceps. A glint in Nathan's eyes suggested that we were on the cusp of something special here.

I hadn't realised it at first but I'd come across Nathan several years ago, back when he was merely a young private school product looking to establish himself in the cut-throat world of grade cricket. Following the completion of his very first match in third grade, Nuggsy had forced Nathan to chug a lukewarm beer in front of the team as an 'initiation'. I watched the seventeen-year-old tearfully choke down the tinned lager in six separate attempts. Nuggsy then proceeded to bark in Nathan's face like a rabid canine, frothing from the mouth before gleefully 'shotgunning' three beers in a row. We all cheered as he stuffed each empty tin into Nathan's kit. It was the kind of humiliation that can make or break a young grade cricketer. Fast forward a few years and Nathan was now a blossoming second grader in his early twenties. A young prodigy, he had yet to truly realise the error of his ways in choosing to cohabitat with fellow grade cricketers (that regret would no doubt come a few years from now). I feared for Nathan's future in a similar way that I envied his ripped jeans, impeccable body-fat percentage and unwavering hairline.

We nailed our remaining beers just as our Uber driver, Brian, arrived in his Volkswagen Polo. In we clambered, four fully grown adult males attempting to contort their bodies into a comically tiny vehicle.

'What the fuck is a bloke like you driving a car like *this*, B?' Nuggsy joked, with just a hint of aggression.

'This is actually my wife's car, Alan,' Brian politely responded.

'Is it? Are your *balls* in the glovebox here too?'

Wholeheartedly committed to the joke, Nuggsy opened the glovebox and began rummaging around for a good thirty seconds in search of Brian's testicles, tossing out a couple of CDs and a car manual in the process. Nuggsy had an Uber passenger rating of 1.7 stars, so it was a surprise Brian had even agreed to pick us up. Certainly he was regretting it now.

'Cir-cuit. Cir-cuit. CIR-CUIT!!' Nuggsy suddenly roared, fists clenched, his eyes lit with a maniacal glint.

He pivoted his body towards the back seat to urge us to join in, grinning insanely so as to expose his cigarette-stained molars. Nathan added to the chant with gusto, his slightly higher voice providing an unintentional harmony, while

I offered a meek rendition of my own. Bruiser, meanwhile, was oblivious to it all, his eyes affixed to his phone, busily texting someone. As the trip continued, the anticipation built to a crescendo. The cab ride (or, nowadays, the Uber ride) to the first bar on the circuit is like nothing on earth. You've had just enough alcohol to loosen your inhibitions to the point where you sincerely believe that this night is actually going to be of some consequence. In the safe confines of this vehicle, surrounded by your best cricket mates, all jokes and elbows, the world (and this night) is your oyster. Who will we see? Where we will go? Will I get arrested? Will I burgle a chop? To those on the outside, you're just four blokes crammed into a Volkswagen Polo being incredibly rude to a bloke who's merely trying to earn a second income to support his young family.

'I'll give *you* five stars if you give *me* five stars!' Nuggsy bellowed through the window as he slammed the door shut, a little harder than he probably should have.

We walked around the corner to our first bar of choice, Freight Lounge. A cursory flash of driver's licences later and in we stepped to a vibrant scene of slowly twisting purple lights, flickering amid the shadowy open-plan set-up.

'Good ratios here, eh?' Bruiser sputtered into my ear.

I don't know where Bruiser was looking—I could only see a handful of females amid the sea of Ralph Lauren and Tommy Hilfiger polos.

'Yeah, mate, there's always good birds here,' I answered, despite not having been at this bar for four years, back when it was trading under a different name and licensee.

Freight was ostensibly a cocktail bar, a groovy place where trust-fund recipients and young property tycoons went to showcase their wealth in front of impressionable and invariably attractive women of good stock. It was not a place where grade cricketers could sit at a table, eat steak and drink schooners of Carlton Draught while watching an NRL match. Every single song had been bastardised and remixed within an inch of its life, to the point where they were essentially indecipherable. That is, until the familiar beat from Drake's 'One Dance' came on, causing many to pick their drinks up and head towards the vacant dancefloor.

I looked over at Nuggsy, who—to my shock—began mouthing the lyrics in perfect sync as he danced his way through the bar. A few years ago it would have taken something near a miracle (or at the very least, the promise of a free beer—also a miracle of sorts) to get him to a place like this. Now he would frequent a bar with a dancefloor and a heavy RnB influence at least once a week. Sure, he'd still go up to the DJ's booth and request 'Khe Sanh' or Elton John's 'Rocket Man', but the very fact that Nuggsy was not only in this place but animatedly lip-syncing Drake's lyrics struck me as a seismic shift in his cultural tastes.

Over on the other side of the bar, Nathan was already deep in conversation with a group of four girls. Tonight—and especially in the favourable Freight Lounge lighting—Nathan was our sugar ticket to a conversation with a human woman. He loosely gripped his Heineken bottle with his thumb and forefinger, showing off the many interlocking wrist bands he'd bargained from a street vendor in Mykonos, his other hand relaxed in the pocket of his ripped skinny jeans. One girl gently stroked his arm; he smiled in a shy, coy manner. He was *in*. That scene was disrupted the moment Nuggsy barged into the middle of the group, carrying a tray holding roughly fourteen tequila shots.

'Oi! Are we gonna bin these, or what?'

'Oh my God! Yes!' the girls cried.

I could see this was what Nuggsy wanted out of Nathan. I had no idea how he paid for the shots; I can only presume a high interest rate credit card was involved. Regardless, the tequila shots went just as quickly as they had come, sending me into a dull haze. The drinks were flying in all directions; the only thing that seemed to be consistent was that Nuggsy always seemed to skip his round. Eventually he got four drinks in, but if I'm being honest, that drink tasted suspiciously like still water.

Soon enough, the four women who had 'fleeced' Nuggsy out of eight tequila shots were now on the dancefloor with four considerably more attractive younger blokes, gyrating their bodies to an eclectic mix of infused sounds from home and abroad.

'We really need to escalate here, lads!' Bruiser chimed in.

Bruiser's eyes were blazing; it was the first time I'd actually seen his eyes that evening, so focused had he been on his iPhone correspondence. His energy had increased tenfold since one of his regular trips to the bathroom, keys still in hand.

'Boys, I'm fucking *blind*! Where should we go next?' Nuggsy roared.

Bruiser stood up from the table, taking charge of the situation.

'I've got a mate who's got a gig later, boys. It's just down the road. Shall we?'

There were few objections from the group. Nathan had been savagely cockblocked, but he didn't seem to mind at all. After all, sex was so easy for him that he'd meet a woman standing in line at the RTA.

'Yeah, this place is shit,' Nuggsy boldly exclaimed, despite proclaiming this 'the best night of my life' just forty-five minutes earlier.

'Alright then, boys, let's go!' Bruiser said. 'I know the guy on the door and I've got a mate behind the bar, so no dramas getting in or paying for drinks.'

Leaving Freight we walked past an endless stream of some of the best-looking girls I had ever seen, patiently standing in line to get in.

'Maybe we should stay for a little bit longer?' I suggested, tilting my head towards the group of scantily clad nineteen-year-olds.

It always seemed to be that the best-looking girls—who I wouldn't even talk to, anyway—were entering a venue just as I was leaving.

'Nah, come on. I've told my mate that we're coming,' Bruiser said, quickly dashing any hopes that one of these girls might stoop three stratospheres down to slum it with me for an evening.

Our next venue on the circuit was The Peruvian. I hadn't been there before, but Bruiser seemed in a hurry to usher us in.

'Come on, lads. We're going to miss the start of the gig!'

We made our way past the seemingly endless velvet ropes towards the front of the queue. Heads down, all focused on our wallets, careful not to fumble our IDs and reveal that we'd been continuously hammering drinks for the past five hours. If asked how many drinks we'd had, the answer would obviously be 'two or three'—the standard response to such a question posed by a bouncer (or a police officer, just prior to undertaking a random breath test).

'Let me do the talking here, lads,' Bruiser said, revelling in the leadership role that had carried over from his time as a senior figure in second grade.

Directly in front of us was a large group of twelve women. Each was wearing a flowery headpiece except for one, who had a silver tiara and matching sash with the word 'BRIDE' splashed across it.

'Are you guys on a hens' night?' Nuggsy asked, a weak attempt to spark conversation.

'No, we just came from a funeral, actually,' one of the girls responded, prompting a raucous cackle from the group.

I couldn't help but laugh at Nuggsy's stupidity. Allowing myself a brief chuckle, I looked up at the girl who had made the joke, to notice she was smiling back at me. At that moment, the ladies were ushered through the door and into the club, promoting us to the front of the line. Bruiser skipped around to greet the exquisitely dressed doorman, standing there with clipboard in hand.

'Siiiiiiiiimonnn! Helloooooooooooo!' Bruiser squealed in a tone I was unfamiliar with.

Nuggsy and I shot a bemused look at each other.

'Gavin? Oh my God! *So* good to see you again!' the bouncer replied, offering a warm hug. 'Have you got tickets for the show? They're starting quite soon.'

'I haven't got tickets, no, but I was hoping you could let me and these good-looking boys in. You know you owe me for the other night!'

Simon rolled his eyes dramatically as he studied Nuggsy and me. Nuggsy was wearing a pair of bulky square-toed shoes that may have passed for fashion in 1997, but looked daggy as fuck when viewed through the prism of modern male footwear trends. His jeans were suitably tight, sure, but that was mainly due to the fact his wallet was so full of gambling receipts and loose shrapnel that it had attracted much of the loose material around the thigh region, which had the effect of creating an unsightly bunch around the crotch area. I wondered whether Nuggsy's ongoing sciatica problems had less to do with his bowling action and more to do with his wallet weighing more than a cricket bat. I hated to think what Nuggsy's reaction would be if the doorman denied him entry on the grounds of his fashion sense.

'Okay, Gavin. Is it just the three of you then?' he asked.

'No, this young lad is with us as well,' Bruiser answered, dragging Nathan under his arm. I noticed Simon's expression brighten instantly.

'Sure, you boys can come in. Enjoy the show, gentlemen!'

Simon unclipped the velvet rope and ushered us in with a tilt of his head.

'Thanks, champ!' Nuggsy blurted as he walked past. He just could not help himself.

Unlike Freight Lounge, this place was completely free of any pretentions whatsoever. Everywhere I looked I saw fun-loving men and women of all ages, shapes and sizes. Again, the ratios weren't great—probably around 80:20 male to female—but this place had good energy. A live band was midway through Ricky Martin's 'She Bangs', working the crowd into a veritable frenzy. All members of the band were shirtless save for the drummer, who was wearing a mesh singlet, skinny jeans and a flamboyant headpiece that may have been culturally insensitive to any Native Americans in attendance.

The dancefloor was calling out to me, though; I yearned for the confidence to join in on the action but, as always, feared my footwork would be found out. As such, I decided to hover on the periphery of the dancefloor and scope the scene out, waiting for the right opportunity to enter the fray. When it comes to nightclub protocol, most men prefer to play the role of the hungry lion standing on the edge of the watering hole, waiting for an opportunity to pounce. Go to any nightclub and you'll see an abundance of single men milling around on the side of the dancefloor, one hand in their hip pocket, the other clasping a schooner of domestic lager, tapping one foot to the beat of the music and bobbing their head at a similar pace, craning their necks in an undignified attempt to establish a connection with someone, anyone. Sadly, eighty per cent of these men will go home having not spoken a single word to a woman that evening, bound by their own crippling self-doubt. If only they had the courage to step onto that dancefloor and flail their arms in the air they might actually end up going home with someone, rather than getting into a fight with another bloke outside a kebab shop at 3 a.m. Say what you will about the lockout laws but I personally think the best way to curb alcohol-related violence is to teach blokes how to dance properly.

I turned around to see where Nathan was, only to bump into a tall gentleman who happened to be walking past at that moment, spilling his drink all over him. Normally this would end badly—I'd have to buy the guy another drink, pay his dry-cleaning bill and avoid eye contact for the rest of the evening—but on this occasion, the bloke took it extremely graciously.

'Don't worry, mate, it happens. Having a good night?' he asked.

I should probably add that the man was shirtless—as it seemed everyone at this venue was. Bruiser hadn't told me about the dress code, but it certainly appeared that shirts were optional. I felt drastically overdressed in my checked collared shirt with ASOS jeans and Oxford shoes.

'Yeah, this place is great!' I answered. 'I'm really sorry about that—can I buy you another?'

'Yeah, sure—let's go!' he said, grabbing my hand and leading me towards the bar.

I found it strange that he grabbed my hand, but I went with it and followed him through the sea of bodies. As we skipped briskly towards the bar, I saw that several couples had paired off and were vigorously making out with one other; a rainbow of tangled skinny jeans, leather jackets and fluoro singlets. Hands cupped the backs of heads and slid down exposed hips and lower backs.

'What are you having?' I asked my new friend.

'Vodka soda for me.'

'Me too!'

We high-fived each other. Just as I'd ordered the round, Bruiser—now shirtless himself—emerged from nowhere to position himself between the two of us.

'Hey, guys!'

'GAVIN!' the shirtless bloke said. 'How are you, big guy?'

It appeared that Bruiser knew everyone in this joint.

'Bruiser, where did you put your shirt?' I asked.

'Coat room, mate. You thinking of getting that big rig out?'

I laughed weakly. My rig was not 'big', nor was I intending on 'getting it out'.

'Yeah, come on—take it off!' Bruiser's mate chimed in.

The drinks arrived and I scurried away, allowing Bruiser and the other bloke to catch up on old times. I turned around to see where the rest of the lads were. Over on the other side of the bar, Nathan was carrying four strawberry daiquiris over to Nuggsy, who was sitting there in a booth by himself. I made my way through the crowd towards them. It was the last song in the band's set—the lights dimmed and the band rested their instruments on the floor. All the focus shifted to the frontman, whose pierced nipples glimmered in the spotlight as he took centre stage.

'This one's for all the *ladies* out there,' he crooned suggestively.

A huge cheer came from the crowd. It wasn't an overly feminine sound—aside from the intermittent squeals from a cluster of bridal parties in attendance—but a male-dominated roar, much like the celebratory sound when someone takes a big wicket to break a dangerous batting partnership. I was beginning to realise that the ratios were even less balanced than I'd initially thought upon entering the venue.

The charismatic frontman shushed the audience down to a complete silence, allowing the keyboardist to take the limelight. The silence was shortlived, however, as Nuggsy leapt to his feet instantly upon hearing the opening F minor chord.

'FUCKING TUUUUNNNE!' he screamed coarsely, eyes blazing like a wildfire.

Nuggsy had immediately identified the song as 'It's Raining Men', based on the opening chord alone. This was one of his greatest pleasures when listening to live music. Whether it was 'To Her Door', 'Take Me Home, Country Roads' or even the 'Queen of the Nile' jingle upon getting a feature on the pokies, Nuggsy always felt compelled to act this way. Half the audience turned around to look at Nuggsy, standing there with strawberry daiquiri in hand, eyes squarely fixed on the slender man on stage. Even the lead singer, who was all but making love to the microphone, opened his eyes and stared towards Nuggsy, allowing himself an imperceptible eyeroll before pressing on.

'Yiiiiiiiiieeeeewwwwwww!!' Nuggsy echoed.

Out of the corner of my eye I saw a fast-moving object making its way towards me. It was the still shirtless Bruiser, who galloped over to whisper into my ear in hushed excitement.

'This is my mate's intro song. They're about to start, come on!'

Bruiser took me by the hand (the second time a man had grabbed my hand in the space of five minutes) and led me to the front of the crowd. Just as we got there, the stage went completely black. The final note of the singer's voice—an F major, if I recall correctly—hung in the air like a top-edged hook shot, allowing the anticipation to build with each passing breath of silent air. Here we were, our hands resting on the front of the stage. I could see the shape of darkened, shadowy figures moving into formation. Next second, the band—now towards the back of the stage, out of view—detonated guitar, drum and bass, showering the entire club with sound, colours and shapes as the stage exploded into light and revealed five men with heads bowed, inexplicably dressed in trench coats. In an instant, all five sprinted towards the front of the stage. They dropped to their knees and—in perfect unison—executed one of the most impressive knee slides I'd seen since Didier Drogba's goal celebration against Barcelona in the 2012 Champions League semifinal. Now, one of the dancers was mere millimetres from me. His left knee had struck my right hand, still resting on the edge of the stage. Without warning, he began thrusting his pelvis towards me, the soft cotton of his suit pants gently slapping my face. He thrust his trench coat open and tore his shirt off, revealing yet another impeccably presented waxed chest. I'd seen dozens of them tonight, but this was certainly the most impressive. The euphoric chorus rang out in all its glory.

Suddenly it all made sense. The hens' party, the cheap daiquiris, the shirtless men, the compliments from strangers, the early-1980s gay anthem. Yes, Bruiser had taken us to a gay bar. I had so many questions. What was this bloke's diet? Was he cutting carbs? What was his training split? But also, why had Bruiser taken us to a gay bar? Bruiser wasn't gay. Well, at least, I was pretty sure that he wasn't. I'd definitely seen him with women before. I was certain he'd been married at one stage. He often liked to send pictures in group text messages of high-priced escorts he would host in his company boardroom after-hours. But perhaps all these things were for show, just Bruiser's way of humouring the grade cricket fraternity with something they could understand, as opposed to something that confronted and challenged them. Did Bruiser lead a secret life? Was he, dare I say it, *happy*? Fuck, he *seemed* happy. Meanwhile, the dancers had ripped their trousers off in one swift movement to reveal Speedos underneath, perfectly in keeping with the theme of the night. I made a mental note to congratulate the choreographer by email on Monday morning.

Anyway, all of these questions would have to wait as, without warning, Bruiser had snuck behind me and hoisted me onto his broad shoulders. There I sat, in full view of the dancefloor, on the shoulders of a treasured former teammate firmly in his element. I raised both my arms out to punch the air as Bruiser bounced me up and down upon his mountainous delts. I could feel every shoulder shrug. Aloft and elated, I swivelled my torso around to look behind at the crowd. To the side of the dancefloor, Nathan was aggressively making out with the bride from the hens' party group. Her tiara had slipped to the side of her head as she leaned into Nathan, her arms around his torso as they twirled in perfect rhythm to the cheesy disco beat.

Her 'BRIDE' sash had fallen onto the floor and now rested on a circle of handbags. Several members of the hens' party were cheering the couple on as Nathan—now resembling a young Patrick Swayze in *Dirty Dancing*—twirled 'Baby' around the dancefloor with effortless style.

But where was Nuggsy? I scanned the room in search of a bald six-foot-two male, normally quite an easy task, yet this particular venue was literally teeming with tall bald blokes. Then, I spotted him over at the bar, talking to a girl—the same girl from the hens' party who'd flashed me a smile at the entrance. Nuggsy had one forearm leaning on the bar, his body language exuding irrational confidence as he (presumably) told the story of his second grade 4-32 in a one dayer—a story that he swore by as a way of 'sealing the deal'. In his mind, he was exhibiting the effortless suave of Clark Gable, but as I looked closer, I was pretty sure the girl was waving in my direction, mouthing the words 'save me'. I scrambled my way down from Bruiser's shoulders and hurried over to the bar.

'Are you okay, big fella? Where the fuck has Bruiser taken us?' I laughed upon joining Nuggsy and his new friend.

In truth, I was having one of the greatest nights of my life but wasn't sure whether I could actually vocalise that yet. There was no denying that Nuggsy was heavily intoxicated. I was confident Nuggsy had never stepped foot in a venue such as this before, but whether it was the forty-seven vodka tonics or something else, he had embraced it wholeheartedly.

'It's fucking going *off* here, mate. Have you met Alex?' he asked, gesturing to the girl next to him.

Nuggsy turned to the barman, using his deepest voice.

'Two big fucking rum and cokes, championship. Wait, make that three.'

'That'll be $47.85, buddy.'

'Oh yeah, we know Bruiser, by the way,' Nuggsy added hastily.

'Bruiser?' the barman asked quizzically.

'Yeah, Bruiser . . . that bloke over there.'

Nuggsy gesticulated back towards the stage. To our surprise, Bruiser had made his way into the show, where he was half-shadow batting and half-dancing to the beat of Eurythmics' 'Sweet Dreams (Are Made of This)'.

'Oh, you mean *Gavin*! You boys call him Bruiser? How cute! No problems, boys, drinks are all taken care of!'

'Yiewwwww! How fucken *good* is this joint?' Nuggsy roared.

'Mate, it's good!'

'You guys haven't been here before?' Alex enquired.

'Nah, why would we come here?' I answered, perhaps a little too quickly.

'Hang on, gotta go take a slash, guys—back soon,' Nuggsy said.

Once Nuggsy was out of earshot, Alex grabbed my arm and drew me close.

'Thanks for coming over—I thought he was never going to stop talking about his Michelle Pfeiffer in second grade, whatever any of that sentence means.'

It had been a while since I'd had a one-on-one conversation with a woman. It was nice to talk about normal things—things that I could never discuss with Nuggsy, Nathan or even Dad. It transpired that Alex and I were enrolled in the same university course. She was only in her early twenties—perhaps ten years younger than me— but, nonetheless, I felt a connection, a spark. Just as we exchanged numbers and agreed to catch up on campus, the bride came running over, tears streaming down her face, clearly regretting the past hour with Nathan.

'Sorry, got a crisis to deal with—let's keep in touch?'

I nodded. As she departed, Nuggsy made his return from the bathroom.

'Scared her off, did ya?' he jibed.

'Nah, mate, she had to leave—Nathan just broke up a marriage before it started.'

'Fuck me, the line for the men's room took a while. Eight blokes came out of the one cubicle! This must be one of those eco-friendly pubs where they save on water.'

Nuggsy shifted into his stool and took a gigantic glug of his rum and coke before turning to face me front-on.

'Mate, to be honest, I'm just happy you're back,' he said, assuming an unusually serious tone.

'Thanks, bud.'

'Honestly, mate, I missed you. I read that whole grand final wrong and I fucked up. I know I fucked up. I just hope I wasn't the reason you quit cricket and left the club. Was I?'

Was he joking?

'No, mate, I left the club because I didn't think my cover drive was good enough to play second grade,' I quipped.

'Really?' Nuggsy asked, eyebrows raised.

'No, of *course* it was because of you, you fucking idiot! We *fixed a fucking match*!'

'Alright, alright. Keep your voice down!' Nuggsy whispered hastily, eyes darting around, as if concerned that someone from the judiciary might be in the room.

'I think we're okay here, Nugget.'

'Well, have you thought at all about coming back?' Nuggsy asked, his blue eyes now impossibly wide, an air of vulnerability creeping in.

'I'm not sure, mate. I mean . . . is there even a spot for me? If so, I think I just want to play with mates in the lower grades. Have those later starts, you know?' I said, lying through my teeth.

The reality was that yes, I *was* interested in making a comeback. Cricket was home to me, and my brief stay with my parents had cemented that in full. In many ways, cricket was all that I knew, comfortable as an old pair of jeans. As far as grade cricket was concerned, I knew all the teams and still recognised most of the players' names from the paper (not to mention the weekly four-hour perusal of MyCricket). I knew where all the grounds were without ever needing Google Maps. I even knew all the umpires. And I knew that if I truly applied myself—well, I could play *at least* second grade again. Truthfully, I missed the taste of the fresh morning air upon arriving at a Saturday home game. The way the hessian was always damp, even when it hadn't rained in three months. I missed the groundsman blowing his cigarette smoke directly in my face when he would tell me, out of the side of his mouth, that it would 'do a bit early' before complaining that the council didn't have enough funds to pay him a decent salary. I missed the sound of Nuggsy's car horn outside my apartment, the rolling of kit wheels across the pavement, the click-clack of spikes en route to the dressing-room. I knew cricket was bad for me, but I had convinced myself long before this night that *I* was good for cricket.

Yes, grade cricket needed me. And I needed it.

'Mate, come down to training at least. Have a chat to the selectors. See how the new stick feels in those tiny mitts of yours,' Nuggsy said, attempting to lighten the mood with a derogatory reference to the size of my hands.

'Alan, look me in the eyes. You have to promise me one thing.'

'I'm still going to bump you in the nets, *cunt*!'

'No. Nuggsy, please. You have to stop match-fixing. I'm never doing that again ... and I'm not having you do it anymore.'

I stopped short of confessing that I hadn't actually thrown that final eighteen months ago, that the outcome was only due to my complete failure as a cricketer, not through any dodgy intention.

Nuggsy looked down at his shoes, polished off his rum and coke with one final swill and loosened his shoulders.

'Alright, legend. Let's do it right this time. No bullshit.'

'Okay, mate. Now, see them off and let's get out of here.'

'We're not leaving yet, mate!'

Just at that moment, the DJ switched gears, the inimitable vocals of Freddie Mercury booming across the room. Every lyric of Queen's 'You're My Best Friend' took on new meaning as we again made our way towards the dancefloor, where Bruiser and Nathan were bopping around in a blur of fist-pumping euphoria.

Together, the four of us linked arms in an all-male semi-circle. Bruiser's vodka and soda spilled onto the shoulder of my checked shirt, but I didn't care.

'Take that shirt off, mate! Get that *big rig* out!' Nuggsy roared.

Fuck it. Why not?

I pulled the wet shirt off and twirled it around in the air, to cheers from the crowd; Nuggsy and Nathan followed suit. My rig was dreadful, fucking ordinary, but it didn't matter. Here we were, four blokes spinning around on the dancefloor, arm in arm, chanting 'LADS, LADS, LADS' as if it were some sort of deity-worshipping ritual, just how we'd always done it back in our cricket days in the sheds after a big win. Nathan's eyes were all but rolling out of his head; he looked in absolute ecstasy. We all were. The band was back together, and tonight was merely the beginning of something special. It didn't get any better than this.

Nuggsy broke away from the semicircle and cavorted over to the bartender to roar his drinks order.

'Same again, championship! We're with Gavin!'

Yeah. Same again.

8

ENLIGHTENMENT

For so long I'd yearned for the chance to start again, to deconstruct and reinvent myself into the person I wanted to be. It's in that spirit that I'd enrolled in university, with the explicit goal of making a positive change in my life. I would study literature and politics at a prestigious university and surround myself with critical thinkers. These would be my enlightenment years. Much like the intellectual and philosophical movement of eighteenth century Europe, I would engage in energetic, spirited discussions about politics, literature, history and science. There would be a free and open exchange of ideas where there was no wrong answer, and where 'out of the box' thinking was encouraged and fostered. A place where I could question the traditional ideas and ways of doing things. In short, the absolute opposite of what I'd been doing for the last decade.

Making any kind of change requires a positive attitude—*intent*—and that was the key word on my mind that first day at university. Decked out in a neatly pressed collared shirt, I had waited patiently at the bus stop for a full sixteen minutes before its arrival, which allowed me 4 overs' worth of shadow batting with my golf umbrella. Unfortunately, I was beaten all ends up on my second ball to one that jagged away sharply, with the third slip taking a good catch low down to his right. But now, just a few weeks later, I'd practically have to sprint to get the bus each morning, despite it being at 10.53 a.m. My sleep-ins were getting longer and longer and my clothes increasingly resembled pyjamas. Hoodies replaced collared shirts; trackpants replaced chinos; thongs replaced loafers. Arriving on campus each morning, however, did fill me with a certain sense of hope—at least for a little while. In contrast to cricket, it was unlikely that hope would kill me here.

I still remember that first day on campus, how the gentle kiss of the late-morning sun cut through the breeze. The trees, mid-blossom, swayed before the sandstone buildings that had hosted some of our society's greatest minds—and tens of thousands of other dropouts. The lawns were impeccably maintained and perfectly symmetrical, not an inch of tatty grass to be seen.

Outfield looks fast.

One of the worrying side effects of spending a lifetime on various sporting fields was that I could no longer view any patch of grass without considering how a ball would run across it. Would it snake? Would I be able to take on the man at mid-off, trusting that it would bobble in his hands before he had a chance to throw the stumps down at the bowler's end? These were unnatural, unhealthy thoughts. But they were there. I'm almost positive that no one else thought of this. To everyone else, this was just a nice, even coverage of couch, a good place to catch up on some readings from the prescribed textbook.

Naturally, just four weeks into my university education I was skipping lectures and tutorials as if they were pre-season beach runs. I'd already missed three tutorials for this class; one more would result in an immediate disqualification from the course. Was I still wasting my life, albeit in new sandstone surroundings? Maybe I should have got that forklift licence Dad was banging on about, after all. At least you can travel with that. My mate Damo, a tradie, realised a couple of years ago that you can walk into sporting stadiums dressed in high-vis and get in free, no questions asked. The security people just assume you're there to fix something. Damo got front-row seats at a sold-out Bruce Springsteen concert just by walking in with a tool belt around his waist and telling everyone he was there to fix a 'sound issue'. It's slightly worrying that tradies can get through any kind of security check without even getting a pat down. I genu-inely hold grave fears that our next major on-shore terrorist attack will be carried out by a bloke wearing a bright orange vest and a hard hat.

I didn't expect to find too many similarities between cricket and university, but as with any social environment there existed a discernible (yet unspoken) hierarchy. Here it was principally based around aesthetics. Jai, a cool-as-fuck nineteen-year-old, was from a creative arts high school in the inner west. His denim shirt was unbuttoned to his navel; his chest appeared to sink inward, indicating a congenital deformity of the anterior thoracic wall. It was strange that he was able to exert such social dominance when he clearly weighed about forty-seven kilograms, but he had women dripping off him. Everything about him was *alternative*. I assumed that his father was a diplomat of some sort, which forced the family to move around and live in various locations like Hong Kong, where he attended an international school and learned how to roll cigarettes with one hand. It was almost a given that he'd lost his virginity at the age of twelve to a Eurasian girl who was now dominating the international modelling circuit. In the context of grade cricket you'd call him a rare unit, but in campus life he was the undisputed Chop King.

So, here I was on a Tuesday at 12.30 p.m., perched at the university bar, midway through my third Carlton Lager. That girl I'd met on the circuit with Nuggsy and Bruiser, Alex, sat opposite me. We'd been hanging out a bit in these first few weeks. Every now and then I felt a pang of guilt about Lara, but then I'd remind myself that she had left me to go and educate impoverished children in Central America. Fucking selfish. Still, I missed her. Anyway, nothing had happened yet between Alex and me, but I was open to it. Unfortunately, this Jai bloke was putting on a real performance. I wasn't sure if I could compete with this skinny-jeaned sex god with the rail-thin physique. He was like a young Mick Jagger, strutting around the bar from table to table, bumming a lighter for his Golden Virginia rollies, dropping in and out of conversations. I noticed Alex glance furtively in his direction and felt a hot rush of jealousy.

It was clear here that all the cool kids gravitated towards each other. Artistic boy-men with enviable hair and effortless charisma. Intelligent young women with unshakeable opinions on literature and socially progressive policy. I'd noticed a couple of other mature age students loitering on the outer and decided to give a wide berth to them lest I risk losing any social capital. One thing was for sure: I felt really fucking old. I was already playing metropolitan under-14s cricket when they were brought into this world. And now, some seventeen or so years later, here we were as equals, their fresh faces acutely juxtaposed with my own sun-damaged visage.

Despite being three schooners deep, I made my way to the lecture theatre for my English literature class. Even though I had missed several tutorials in succession, this was, without doubt, my most cherished of subjects. It afforded me the opportunity to consider the views of some of my favourite authors in an environment not dissimilar to book club, where I had first met Lara all those years ago. Of course, if it was revealed to my then teammates that I was in a book club I risked the admonishment of my peers—a collection of individuals who I fucking hated anyway, but whose validation I lived and died by. It was really only by chance and a degree of blackmail that I was able to keep that a secret for as long as I did. But there was no judgement here. Finally I was free to adore the works of Shakespeare, to marvel at the precision of Hemingway, to consider the philosophy of Kierkegaard. It was a welcome change, as very few of my grade cricket teammates were able to discuss literature, although I guess a couple of the younger kids had read the Harry Potter series. To be honest, I've never really been into the fantasy genre; to me, the most unbelievable part of the Harry Potter series isn't the magic stuff—it's the fact that a weak, bespectacled kid with a visible scar and small hands has somehow been elevated to alpha male of an entire school.

As part of our first module for English literature, the class was tasked with a group assignment, which is literally the worst type of assignment there is. Cricket, in many ways, is basically an extended group assignment: one person does all the work and the others just climb on board. Anyway, I saw this as the perfect opportunity to be grouped with Alex, to get closer to her, and to sneak a decent grade from her work. I had training this afternoon, cricket on Saturdays and was always fairly hungover on Sundays, thanks to my new living situation, so I needed her help.

Just as I was about to turn to Alex and ask her to be my group partner, I noticed Jai making his way over from the other side of the room. Alex's body language immediately shifted: she sat up in her chair, completely upright, chest out, exuding approachability. Jai propped one leg up on the chair in front of her—channelling the Danny Zuko character in *Grease*—and gazed into her eyes. His jeans were impossibly tight; it was as if he had a million rubber bands strapped around his inner thighs.

'So, I'm thinking you and me should do it together,' Jai murmured seductively.

I realised I needed to interject now, lest Alex fall even deeper into his emerald eyes.

'Nah, it's all good, champ,' I blurted.

'Excuse me?'

'Alex and I are going to work on this one. I think there's a few people over there still looking for a partner.'

I gesticulated toward the front corner of the lecture hall, where a collection of social outcasts stood.

'Is that right?' Jai replied, his eyes still transfixed upon Alex. It was like he was putting her under a spell.

Jai's answer sent me into full 'catcher behind the wicket' mode. Without explanation, I unleashed a series of cricket sledges that would normally be directed at opposition batsmen but were now being applied out of context and targeted at a defiantly anti-sport hipster.

'Come on here, lads! This bloke's got no idea! Someone get this bloke a gym membership! *One brings two!*'

It worked, I had thrown him. He unlocked his eyes from Alex and looked at me with a bemused expression, the same look that Lara had given me the first time I tried to explain the LBW law.

'Um . . . I think I'm going to . . . um . . . yeah,' he stuttered, taking his leg down from the chair and backing away into the arms of fifteen attractive girls, each of whom was eager to do a 'group project' with him.

I looked over at Alex, whose gaze followed Jai for a moment before she turned to me with wide eyes, as if the absurd exchange had never taken place.

'So, we should pair up!'

I checked my phone to read three imaginary notifications.

'Sure, I mean, only if you want to.'

'I can go with someone else if you'd pref—'

'No, no!' I immediately interrupted. 'Together. Together is fine. It's gonna be great. Let's meet up after class and get started. See you at the lawn?'

We were tasked with discussing some of Shakespeare's most pertinent themes in any one of his major works. It was a broad description that, really, spoke to how difficult it was to fail this Arts degree. 'Write about anything you want; just don't fuck it up and we'll give you at least a credit,' was more or less the brief.

Alex unfolded a large picnic blanket, handing me a corner so we could lay it down evenly.

'Get the covers on!' I said wittily.

'What?'

'Just a little cricket joke.'

'Argh, literally the worst sport ever. My dad loves it. I just do not get it.'

My heart broke into a thousand tiny pieces.

As we sat down, I ran my fingers over the blades of grass, marvelling in its texture, lost in its perfection. It was the best coverage of grass I'd seen since my season in England many years back, where I'd discovered it was almost impossible to misfield a ball. Meanwhile, Alex had pulled out books and printed readings. Her mind was clearly on nailing this group assignment.

'Okay, so where do you think we should start?' she asked.

With one eye on my watch to ensure I made it to training on time, I made the executive decision to leave all of the heavy lifting to Alex. As much as I was enjoying spending time with this girl, my true mistress—grade cricket—was waiting for me elsewhere. Then, out of nowhere, Nuggsy's gruff voice popped into my head.

Yeah, she's waiting to fuck you!

I stifled a snigger at the thought that grade cricket was my mistress and waiting to have sex with me again. Like an incessant ex-girlfriend you know is no good for you, but you keep going back to her anyway. Why? Well, because it's all you've ever known and you have a deep-seated fear of change.

'What's so funny?' Alex said.

'Oh, never mind. Just thinking about this meme I saw the other day.'

'Oh my God, I love memes!' Alex smiled, placing a hand on my arm, visibly excited that we shared an enjoyment of pictures with funny captions found on the internet.

Okay, I'll stay here for a bit longer.

'Maybe we should start with the most obvious one— *Romeo and Juliet?* The battle between love and hate, between fate and free will.'

The more Alex spoke about Shakespearean themes, the more I realised how applicable they were to cricket. I had my own love–hate relationship with the game, in much the same way the Capulet and Montague families did with each other. Not as many deaths, though, plus the language was a little rougher. But the constant selection issues a club would face between an ageing (23-year-old) batsman and an up-and-coming (20-year-old) talent were evident.

'And then there's *The Tempest*,' she continued, 'which looks at reconciliation versus forgiveness, the idea of nature versus nurture in raising children, while also exploring topics around magic, sleep and dreams. Hey, did you know the phrase "the stuff dreams are made of" comes from this play?'

No, I didn't know that. All I knew was that last night I'd dreamed that I couldn't get my pads on in time. I hadn't had that dream in years, but the very prospect of playing again had brought it all back to me. I was batting six and a few wickets had fallen in quick succession. I'd raced to the sheds to put my pads on, but the velcro straps weren't holding. I'd looked around for my bat but it was nowhere to be found. None of my teammates were willing to let me borrow theirs, so I'd asked the outgoing batsman, Damo, if I could borrow his, but he was too busy steaming past me. There I stood on the corner of the field, pads loose around my ankles, imploring the umpire to give me more time to source a cricket bat. With a menacing grin, the umpire raised his finger slowly, mouthing the words 'timed out' while tilting his other wrist towards his eyes as if looking at a watch. At that moment, I'd woken up in the coldest of sweats. Did Shakespeare tackle any of that in *The Tempest?* I wondered if this would be useful for the group project.

'No, I didn't know that, Alex,' I finally responded.

'Well, what about *Othello?* I mean, the big ones there are jealousy and self-deception . . .'

I thought to myself about how I came across self-deception on a weekly basis in grade cricket, but decided against sharing that with Alex. Again, I stole a quick look at my watch.

Training's on soon. Can't be late. Need to get an early hit.

'Hey, what brand is that?' Alex enquired, having seen me check the time.

She grabbed my wrist to investigate the watch face in detail. While it had been a thirtieth birthday present from Lara, I had no idea what brand it was. She'd sourced it from some Italian-based watchmaker at great expense. I was sceptical of the gesture since I assumed it was her way of saying 'here's an extremely rare, expensive piece of jewellery that I've gone to great lengths to procure, on the understanding that you will be issuing me an engagement ring within the next six to twelve months'. At least, that's what my mates were telling me, and who was I to think differently? In retrospect, I should have just taken it for what it was: a thoughtful present from a woman who loved me. No real agenda, just something that people in loving, long-term relationships do for one another, I guess.

Immediately, I felt guilty for using this treasured time-piece to flirt clumsily with a different girl. To be honest, though, I was confused by Alex's demeanour. Just a few short hours ago she was lost in the eyes of a bloke named Jai, who had weak forearms and no rig; now, she was holding my wrist up so close that her breath was fogging up the Italian-made watch face. I quickly pulled away and de-fogged the face, lest I be late for training on account of losing track of time.

'I . . . I have to go,' I mumbled awkwardly. Truth be told, I was not ready for this.

Alex instantly let go of my hand and recoiled to the other side of the blanket, arms crossed, visibly embarrassed. My crude rejection must have been particularly hurtful coming from a considerably less attractive human, one ten years her senior. Just as the awkward moment played out, a group of young, virile rugby jocks happened to walk past us, identically dressed in their university-branded polos, Canterbury rugby shorts and boat shoes. I watched as their eyes lingered on Alex before settling on me, bemused at the pairing.

'Isn't that someone's dad?' one mock-whispered loudly.

I bowed my head, alpha'd by a group of nineteen-year-old boy-men who'd presumably had more sex in the first few weeks of this semester than I'd managed in the past twelve months. What's more, I couldn't help but notice they were on their way towards the economics centre, which meant they were probably in their first or second year of a commerce degree, something I knew required an ATAR in the mid-nineties. So not only were these blokes younger, better-looking and more sexually accomplished than me, but they were more intelligent too.

I needed to take some anger out.

I'd better get to training.

9

THE COMEBACK

Arriving early for my first training session had afforded me a chance to reflect on all the good times I'd had here over the years, much in the same way the main character of a Hollywood sports movie will go to the stadium the night before the big match and breathe in all that is before them. When watching such movies, I always wondered whether it was cost-effective for these stadia to always be open, at all hours, with all the lights on and a solitary, random cleaner sweeping the aisles. Seemed like this could also potentially be a big contributor to global warming, another issue never far from my mind now that I was studying at university.

Despite being early, I was experienced enough to know one should never enter the complex until the nets have been fully erected. After all, the putting up and taking down of cricket nets is a physically arduous and intellectually sapping process best left to club officials and brown-nosing juniors. I may have been away from the game a little while but I hadn't forgotten the unwritten rules of grade cricket. From behind the toilet block I peeked out to watch a series of P-plate drivers roll up and park directly behind the nets. These were mainly cheap, colourful offerings from Asian car makers, but the occasional European model would arrive, suggesting that someone in the family had a well-paid job, and affording them the luxury of feeling like they've 'made it' for fifteen minutes while they drive to training.

Speaking of cars, it was then that Nuggsy's yellowing 1994 Nissan Pulsar turned the corner. His bald head was half out of the window, attempting to get full optics of his surrounds as he entered the car park. With one arm out leaning on the driver's side windowsill, Nuggsy threw his handbrake on to perform a *Tokyo Drift*-style manoeuvre into the car park. I made my way around from the toilet block into Nuggsy's direct line of vision.

'Ayyyyyy! It's the big fella!' he exclaimed loudly, as he stepped out from the car.

A couple of passers-by on an evening walk with their dog stopped to look at me, as if Nuggsy was at a trade fair, summoning the crowd to view something spectacular.

'He's back, boys! Lock up your mums!' Nuggsy bellowed before jabbing me in the ribs several times.

Suddenly I was back to exactly where I was just eighteen months ago. As always, all eyes were on Nuggsy. He popped open the boot of his car to retrieve his kit, unleashing a smell that would have caused even the steeliest war veteran to weep. There must have been a dozen pie wrappers in the back, three of which escaped in the afternoon breeze. A Venetian rug was also rolled tightly in the back. I dared not ask what was in it.

'Alright, who's giving me some fucking throw downs?' cried Nuggsy, more as a statement than a question.

Naturally, given Nuggsy's status at the club, there were more than a few takers. A fresh-faced seventeen-year-old tentatively put his hand up.

'I'll give you some if you give me a few rounds too?' he proffered naively.

Little did the kid know that not only was he never going to be getting any throw downs, it was more than likely that his shoulder would be so sore from completing the task that he'd be unavailable for the next month due to tendonitis.

I'd noticed Bobby, an elderly scorer who'd been associated with the club for close to fifty years, was writing down the names of the players who were in attendance, fastidiously noting their arrival times and thereby calculating the order they would be put into the nets.

'Bobby! Long time no see!'

'I don't believe it. I don't believe what I'm seeing,' Bobby replied, genuinely stunned to see me.

From being the occasional fourth grade scorer, to re-marking the lines on the wicket, to picking up the mountains of dog shit left by local canines before each Saturday, Bobby lived and died through his involvement with the club. He resided in a retirement village in the same suburb as the club's home ground and openly revelled in being among 'fit, athletic boys'.

'Where on earth have you been?' asked Bobby.

'Well, I actually—'

'Hang on a moment,' he interjected, scribbling something down on his notepad. 'Jonesy's just turned up.'

This was typical of grade cricket clubs. No one cares what you're up to outside of grade cricket. It doesn't matter what you are doing with your life, if you're applying for a new job, thinking about entering the property market, looking to start a family, or have saved a rescue dog and given it a new home. To grade cricketers and club officials, your entire life revolves around how well you hit a cover drive and whether you attend training—including club functions, official or otherwise—on a regular basis. There was always a complete lack of understanding about how real life worked beyond grade cricket, and nowhere was that more evident than at club practice.

Firstly, if you can't get to training at 4 p.m. on a Tuesday afternoon, you'll either be a) publicly admonished or b) simply not selected. To those with jobs, this is a very difficult situation to negotiate. If you've ever taken a 'mental-health day' and decided to go to a Westfield, or perhaps another precinct where large collections of people are just out in the world, it's impossible not to think, 'Why aren't these people at work?' But in grade cricket, if you aren't putting cricket first—before your career, before your education, your relationships—you can, and will, be punished. Sure, this sort of attitude might be acceptable when you're on the fringe of an Ashes call-up or even on the outskirts of a state selection as a 20-year-old, but for a 31-year-old who just wants to play a bit of competitive cricket on a Saturday, it's fucking overkill.

Give up everything for cricket or be happy.

Lara had often asked me what guys in my team did outside of cricket. She always seemed disappointed when I struggled to answer this very simple question. Because of her, I'd subsequently resolved to ask each team member what they were doing and make a mental note of it. Goes without saying that I didn't really give a shit what some bloke in twos was doing for a crust. He could have raised forty thousand dollars for breast cancer research by climbing Mount Kilimanjaro for all I knew, but if he was consistently pushing them down the leg side, he was dead to me. But Lara always knew every single detail about her friends, even her friends-of-friends. It was more socially acceptable for two women to go for a coffee and talk for hours, gazing into each other's eyes, gleaning all the ins and outs of the human experience. For men, we always had to be 'doing' something, even if that meant sitting next to each other and getting drunk in a bar, watching some form of televised sport. Again, even if a meaningful conversation between two men did take place in this environment, the excessive consumption of alcohol would have created large blackspots in the participants' memory, rendering all the content forgotten within the space of twelve hours.

'Why don't you get your pads on now?' Bobby suggested. 'We'll get you in early.'

This was one of the greatest honours that could be bestowed on any person at training. *An early hit.* As all cricketers know, the sweet spot at training is to get into either the second or third batting group. The first batting group is always subjected to a handful of top-order batsmen bowling experimental finger spin and/or sixth grade train-on squad bowlers under the age of seventeen. The first batting group is therefore no better equipped for the weekend ahead, after facing ten minutes of bowling that John Howard himself would describe as weak. In fact, they're probably worse off for the experience.

But by the time the second and third groups go in, more people have arrived at training, there is a better calibre of bowling and—crucially—the sun is still up. Put simply, if you aren't able to knock off work before 4 p.m. then good luck fighting peak-hour traffic to get there before 6.30 p.m., at which point your ten minutes largely turns into an exercise in minimising your thigh bruise count to under five.

I walked over to my kit, shaking hands with just about every person I used to know from the club. There were dozens of new faces among the crowd but I was wary of engaging anybody who I wasn't sure could directly offer me something. I unzipped my kit for the first time at a practice that summer.

Left pad on first. Always left pad on first.

Now in full kit, I felt complete. As the first batting group got the call of 'last six' from Bobby, my nerves began to jangle. Aside from that Fathers vs Sons match (where they used a compo ball), I hadn't faced a cricket ball in eighteen months. Sure, I'd scored the odd 'pretty 30' in front of the mirror and at a couple of bus stops with an umbrella, but it was significantly harder to hit a cricket ball hurtling down at you at around 115 k's per hour.

'In you go, son!' Bobby announced.

As I walked down the net, the outgoing batsman shot me a sickly look, as if to confirm the next ten minutes of net batting would be essentially a matter of survival. Upon facing up, I noticed Nuggsy shuffle over from the first net into the middle net—my net. Nuggsy was a one-time first grade bowler who, despite his advancing years, still boasted all the necessary attributes required to expose a batting fraud like me. He would have me in trouble even if I was in the most sparkling form of my life, let alone fresh off an eighteen-month sabbatical. But first, a third grader by the name Javagal, a part-time medium pacer, had the honour of serving up my first pill. He steamed in, his limbs an epileptic blur of rhythm and energy. The ball seemed to trickle out of his cocked wrist, full and easily driveable. I pressed my front foot towards the pitch of the ball, transferring my body weight from waist and shoulders through my front arm and elbow, extending the wrist and forearms through the line of the ball.

And I fucking middled it.

'That's four, champ!' I instantly cried out to Javagal, a man I'd never met nor spoken to before.

Next up was second grade leg spinner Scotty, who dragged one down to present me with an appetising half-tracker. I moved back and away, giving myself a little bit of room and exposing all three stumps as I fully exploited the depth of the crease, dropping my hands through the ball and lashing a glorious square cut.

Was cricket always this easy?

Scotty's trash was swiftly followed by more garbage, this time courtesy of Macca, the 41-year-old fourth grade opening 'quick'. As he strayed into a leg-side line, I morphed into a combination of V.V.S. Laxman and Michael Vaughan, whipping the ball through mid-wicket off my pads for another perfectly timed boundary.

'Fuck, good start from you!' called down Macca.

'Mate, if there's one thing you need to take away from today it's that you can't bowl on my legs!'

Throughout my impressive opening, Nuggsy had remained standing at the top of his mark, biding his time. Finally, with dozens of eyes on him, Nuggsy commenced his run-up, a short three-paced walk before engaging his mountainous glutes and springing into an energetic canter, which evolved into a gallop just as he approached the crease. I could see the happiness in his eyes as he exploded into his jump. I should have been watching the seam but I was strangely transfixed by his face. The perfect presentation of Nuggsy's seam was a thing of beauty, poetry in motion. And as I'd expected, this was the first decent ball I'd faced since my return to grade cricket. It pitched on a good length on the off stump before savagely jagging in towards my exposed thigh. Almost instantaneously, pink and purple bruising began to show, small bite marks from the seam perfectly imprinted onto the skin.

'Don't rub it! Don't rub it!!' Nuggsy howled hysterically.

The ball had trickled down to the middle of the pitch, which had triggered a Mexican stand-off. Who would be the one to move forward and get it? Me, the batsman, who had just been struck in the thigh, currently reeling in agony? Or Nuggsy, the bowler, who was busily feasting on the subsequent euphoria that comes from causing physical pain to a batsman? Whenever a ball settles in the middle of the pitch, what happens next tells you everything you need to know about both people. Some thirty seconds passed before I couldn't bear it any longer and dashed down the wicket to retrieve the ball. As suspected, a two piecer. I'd noticed this ball in Nuggsy's room the first day I'd moved in, actually. It had been positioned on the mantelpiece next to a large vanilla-scented candle, positively glowing. Nuggsy had shined that ball every day since it was given to him as a gift for Christmas 2011, which explained the extravagant swing, extra pace and pronounced seam movement.

Despite that early hiccup, the rest of the net couldn't have gone much better. Walking out, I proceeded to thank the bowlers for bowling at me, such was my confidence. This was common courtesy for their toil and hard work on what was a warm Tuesday afternoon, but more importantly it was to mark myself as a good, strong bloke. By the time it was Nuggsy's turn to have a hit, the sun had well and truly faded into the night sky.

During my time away from the game, our club had gone through a drastic change of personnel, both on and off the field. The ageing committee members had been replaced by a younger generation of prominent businessmen, all of whom had sons with aspirations of playing first grade. It was abundantly clear they were abusing their positions to act as lobbyists for their sons' cricketing ambitions.

Anyway, standing with his pads on behind the first net, Nuggsy was engaged in a seemingly important conversation with Sean Kline, part of the in-house legal counsel for one of the country's biggest banks. Kline was a fucking power player; he wore a suit, *sans* tie, and just looked the business. His son, Shane, was an abysmal cricketer, but had 'somehow' managed to find himself batting at four in second grade.

'What do you mean third grade?' Nuggsy screamed, recoiling back in shock.

Training all but stopped as Nuggsy embarked on an epic tirade. 'You're telling me that Shane is going to keep his place in twos and you're fucking me off down with the plebs in threes? I've given my *life* to this fucking club! And for what? For some fuckwit in a suit to tell me that Daddy is looking after his son so he can go home and get blown by his trophy wife? It's cunts like you that make me want to fucking end it all!'

To his credit, Sean was doing his best to console Alan in this moment of rage, despite the flurry of increasingly obscene insults. He attempted to place a hand on his shoulder, intending to escort him to a more discreet location to talk it through, but that didn't go down well at all.

'Don't fucking touch me, *champ*. This fucking shoulder has got a right to put itself through your chin.'

I was now frozen in time, standing two metres away from a suited businessman who was being verbally abused by a bloke with ash stains all over his singlet.

'I'm sorry, Alan, the selection panel just feels it's best for the *balance* of the side this week. Look, get in the nets now, have a hit and *work hard*.'

Nuggsy stormed off, cursing under his breath as he made his way into the first net.

'Ah, hang on, Nuggsy, we'll actually need you in the third net tonight,' Bobby belatedly called out.

Nuggsy stood still, already halfway down the first net. He looked directly in the eyes at Bobby, who was now cowering behind his clipboard in fright, before finally trudging over to the third net. Let's be clear: the third net is where cricket goes to die. It's as close to park cricket as you will see in the grade sphere. Here, random blokes in full whites and black sports shoes attempt various forms of wizardry, often in subcontinental style, and usually very poorly. It's a place where desperately out of form batsmen who've never bowled a ball in a match suddenly transform into precocious leg spinners, albeit ones who hit the side net two out of three deliveries. This is why the third net is often referred to as 'the shit net', and for good reason. It's directly comparable to bin juice. The dregs of cricket and society, together in a single net.

Nuggsy scratched the crease with the front spike of his right boot, a token attempt to take guard. I could hear him shout the words 'fuck *me*' as some middling nobody with an aesthetically offensive mixed action rolled up to deliver his first ball. He pressed forward looking to defend, only to be beaten all ends up. Despite the delivery only being in the vicinity of 100 k's, his off stump catapulted through the back net as if he'd just copped a 160 kilometre per hour bullet from Shoaib Akhtar. This was all too much for Nuggsy to take. This wasn't just a man at his wit's end, this was Mount Vesuvius on the brink of eruption, and those who had decided to attend training that day were the town of Pompeii. His reaction was predictably visceral.

'Farrrrkkk!' Nuggsy screamed.

The whole training ground stopped. Bowlers stopped bowling, fielding drills ceased, balls suspended in mid-air. Nuggsy turned around and, with the flourish of a samurai, demolished both remaining stumps out of the ground with a horizontal bat swipe; the cleanest connection he'd made in weeks.

'This. Club. Is. Fucking. *Fucked!*'

Players parted as Nuggsy stormed out of the net in a violent fury, gripping his bat like an axe, shrieking profanities at the top of his voice. His final act of aggression was to snap his bat over a nearby park bench, the crack of the blade echoing through the now eerily quiet suburb. He got in his car, still fully padded up with his lid on, and wound down the window.

'I'm going to burn these nets and this *fucking club down!*' he yelled, letting out a comically evil laugh as he sped off into the distance.

This was apparently the fourth time he'd threatened to torch the nets this season, so no one really believed he was an arsonist. What I did know was that Nuggsy was playing third grade this week, and that suited me. Having nailed a few cover drives, a couple of elegant whips off the pads and one delightful sweep shot, I had secured my own position in thirds, where I'd be batting six.

Yes, Nuggsy and I would turn up together on Saturday, just like old times, and do it all again.

I waited outside on the street for Nuggsy, just as I'd always done throughout our grade cricket lifetime. Even though we were now living under the same roof, tradition was tradition, and I couldn't imagine kicking off a Saturday of grade cricket any other way. I'd always loved those anxious moments, waiting for Nuggsy to pull up alongside the kerb in his beat-up Nissan Pulsar, crudely honking the horn to piss off my neighbours and mark the commencement of the day's proceedings. Would he get here on time? Had he been pulled over by an RBT on his way to pick me up—and if so, should I expect a phone call from the police? And how much was bail again? Four hundred dollars? Five hundred?

Nuggsy eventually opened the front door, still shirtless, a piece of toast in his mouth, kit hoisted over his right shoulder. He carefully eased himself out of the house so as not to wedge himself in the doorway, before strolling towards the car and hauling his kit into the boot.

'Ready to go, big dog?' I asked Nuggsy. Opening the car door, he threw his entire body weight, with unnecessary additional force, into the driver's seat, fully testing what was left of the car's wearing suspension. He reached over and unlocked the passenger door, his car predictably lacking a central locking feature.

'Mate, how good? Not a cloud in the sky, the sun is shining ... we're going to *smash* these blokes today. I'm feeling good for a few poles and you're going to get some runs! How good.'

The final 'how good' was not framed as a question but an unambiguous statement. With all parties now buckled and ready to go, he pressed play on his stereo system, worth approximately three times the value of the car itself. Fortuitously, Thin Lizzy's 'The Boys are Back in Town' began to blare. I wondered whether he had gone to the trouble of teeing this song up in advance, a nice touch to mark our grade cricket reunion, but I suspected that would be giving his organisational skills too much credit.

He was already midway through his first cigarette, the third of the morning. Despite his cashflow issues, Nuggsy was still dolling out around a hundred bucks a week on durries. Smoke filled the vehicle, causing me to descend into a coughing fit. Noticing my discomfort, he thrust his hand down the driver's side door and began to manually wind his window down. His left forearm rested on the top of the wheel, his right arm hung out of the window, a trail of smoke mapping our path like a grey flare along the streets of suburbia. I shuffled my feet through the sea of empty chocolate milk cartons and cardboard sandwich cases.

'Feels good to be back, Nuggler,' I said, coughing through the smoke but feeding off his energy.

Nuggsy, dropped from second grade for this match, had been keen to show he had status by rolling up late. He entered the dressing-room with a Sausage & Egg McMuffin and McCafe cappuccino in his hands. Despite our late arrival, I was still able to nab my old seat in the dressing-room. Nuggsy wasn't so lucky, although they say you make your own luck, which is what led him to remove four kits from their seats and chuck them into the middle of the room, allowing him to claim prime position. The corner seat is the most coveted position in the entire dressing-room, with perhaps the exception of the abandoned physio table.

The bloke brave enough to hop onto the physio table is afforded the finest of optics, while making it impossible for his teammates to avoid looking at his crotch region.

The corner seat's benefits can best be understood as a mathematical equation, whereby one acquires more real estate for the same fixed price of admission. Without delving heavily into the fundamentals of Pythagoras's theorem (although I guess there's not a lot to it, really, is there? Fucking $a^2 + b^2 = c^2$? You're telling me that's a *theory*?), it essentially boils down to being able to spread your legs as far apart as you like. This is particularly helpful when you're chaffing badly after a full day in the field. What's more, there's still plenty of space for your kit, your circuit bag, your circuit shirt and your towel. Fucking *good areas*, indeed.

As the captain rattled off the classics—'work hard,' 'work the singles, 'bat time' and 'play the ball on its merits'— I closed my eyes and thought about how far I'd come. The answer came to me with frightening speed: not that far. I don't know why but I'd thought my return would be more glamorous than this. Had I made a horrible mistake in returning to grade cricket?

All my long-forgotten fears began to rush back to the forefront of my mind. We'd won the toss and elected to bat on a frighteningly hard, flat deck. I've always found it interesting when commentators suggest a batsman would be 'licking his lips' at the prospect of batting on such a deck. Conversely, it implies that batsmen are only ever nervous when the conditions favour the fielding side, conjuring imagery of a 1980s-era West Indian attack marking out their run. No, this is never the case. We're always fucking scared, regardless of the state of the deck. I could be batting on the Hume Highway against a 45-year-old slow medium bowler and I'd still be wondering if one will jag back in to publicly humiliate me in front of friends and family. More to the point, I've never seen a batsman licking their lips at anything, unless we're talking about Dazza at the strippers on that end of season circuit a few years ago.

We walked out from the dressing-rooms and sat in front of the pavilion. The sun shone brightly overhead as a solitary dog walker closed the metal fence that circled the ground. At least someone was enjoying the day. The click-clacking of spikes on concrete mixed with the sounds of back slapping and swigged water bottles as the collection of nameless young men entered the field of play. Our pavilion hadn't changed much over the years. The adage of 'if it ain't broke, don't fix it' couldn't be more appropriate for our club, where money was lavished on poorly performing first graders and new training balls at the expense of essential infrastructure upgrades. The paint on the wooden benches wilted like a tired outfielder in the unforgiving sun; the floorboards creaked underfoot; the memorabilia was tremendously dated. The whole point of this memorabilia was to exemplify to visitors the proud history of this once strong club, but in reality it was a stark reminder that little on-field success had come our way since second grade made the final back in 1971.

We sat there, waiting for the umpire to call play. I was batting at six, which meant I was still in my training kit. Whenever I batted six, I liked to start watching in my training kit before switching to my whites when the first wicket fell. When we were two down, that was my cue to put my pads on. Incremental preparation. Then, when the third wicket fell, I'd go in and put the rest of it on—thigh pad, box and gloves—and sit back down clutching my helmet, praying for a 300-run partnership. Meanwhile, Nuggsy was scrolling through his phone, both legs elevated on a plastic chair as he reclined on one of the wooden benches set aside for the players.

'I'd get your pads on if I was you,' he whispered out of the corner of his mouth.

As mentioned, I'm a big believer in showing faith in your batsmen by leaving padding up until the last minute, but I couldn't help feeling that Nuggsy was foreshadowing something.

'Fuck me, mate, you haven't fixed this one, have you?'

'Nah, mate,' he laughed. 'These blokes are just fucking shithouse.'

The bowler steamed in, a hurricane of arms and legs. Our opening batsman pressed forward and comfortably defended to mid-off.

'P'oh! This is a fucking road!' cried Robbo, judging the conditions based on the first ball of the day.

'Nice day to watch some cricket, don't you reckon, Nuggler?' I said, slapping Nuggsy's leg.

He raised one eyebrow at me, like the oracle he often was. The second ball of the innings mirrored the first, except this time our opening batsman had decided to disobey the oft spoken but rarely adhered to rule of 'playing in the V early'. He wandered across his stumps and attempted the most extravagant of lofted, leg-side whips, only to be trapped dead in front. The ball hit the 'fleshy' part of the pad, the region that offers the most protection available, causing the ball to roll gently back to the bowler.

'That's fucking plumb!' Nuggsy called out, even before the umpire could raise his finger. 'Go on, mate, I told you! Get 'em on!'

I turned and made my way to the pavilion. As always, old routines took over, as if my faculties knew I was back playing cricket again, and I found myself in desperate need of the bathroom. Just as I lifted the lid of the toilet bowl I heard another loud, prolonged appeal, followed by the discordant squeals of eleven adult men.

Fuck, that was quick. Two down already. This wicket must be fucked.

I flushed the toilet and returned to the sheds to chuck my kit on. I was now doing this in the presence of two freshly dismissed batsmen, who were facing the crushing realisation that they'd wasted yet another Saturday. It was barely 10.30 a.m. yet their match was over—and their weekend, consequently, ruined. The best they could hope for now was for us to get rolled cheaply. And if one of their batsman had a nice-looking cover drive, then maybe we could feed for a couple of hours too. Small victories.

As I strapped my pads on, I was overwhelmed by yet another massive shout.

'Ah, for fuck's sake!' cried somebody, followed by the unmistakable sound of a plastic chair being upended.

It is happening. I'll be out in the middle in no time. This is real.

Rambo and Briggsy began to rebuild the innings, putting together a decent little partnership. It's always the way, isn't it? Just when you're ready to go in, your teammates start to exhibit uncharacteristic mettle. I sat there, full kit on—pads, thigh pad, chest guard, armguard, gloves, helmet—almost willing a wicket to fall, but my teammates were holding firm, manfully steering us into safe waters. All of a sudden, the bowling looked remarkably pedestrian. A few misfields here and there, a couple of back-to-back boundaries, and we were back on top. Even the chat had begun to dissipate. The opposition's lack of energy was inversely proportional to our own sudden spike in energy. It goes without saying that both teams cannot have the same amount of energy at the same time, for there is a finite amount of energy on a cricket field. Just twenty minutes ago they were literally roaring with self-belief, but Rambo and Briggsy had stolen all the momentum. This momentum extended to the pavilion, where we were becoming bullishly vocal in our support. As always, this placed me in a difficult predicament. When you come to the wicket at, say, 4-20, after a flurry of wickets, you've got very little to lose. People's expectations are low. You can play it one of two ways: grit it out and soak up as many balls as possible, so that you can return to the pavilion and receive plaudits for your defiant innings in the face of adversity, or give yourself a licence to tee off and earn some quick runs. The second scenario is a win-win, in the sense that if you get out you can blame the batsmen before you for failing to lay a platform. It's their fault, not yours. And if, by some stroke of fortune, you do manage to pile on 30 or 40 runs, well, you're a hero.

All these thoughts were running through my head the moment Rambo popped one back to the bowler, leaving us at 4-75. It made my decision even harder, for while 4-75 is in no way a solid platform, neither is it embarrassingly poor. Yes, it's a pretty shit start by professional standards—a commentator would describe the session as a 'clear win to the bowling team'—but in the grade cricket sphere, 4-75 actually isn't too bad. A bad start would be, say, 4-23, the kind of start that sees you get rolled for a total of 75 runs. To make things worse, your number eleven will top score with 23 not out, which gives him the right to vociferously opine how easy the conditions were, and that he should be given an immediate promotion up the batting order based on his contribution (even though 20 of his runs came from inside edges). But with just four wickets down, and 75 valuable runs already on the board, I wouldn't be able to just tee off and blame my predecessors for my inevitable failure. No, I would have to fail a different way.

In that respect, I managed to nail the brief, for my innings passed without much fanfare. Really, it was no different from every other innings I'd ever played in grade cricket. I'd started quite confidently, pushing a few quick singles, even clipping a nice boundary off my pads to get things underway. For a moment, and it's embarrassing to admit this, I honestly believed that this was going to be 'my day'. But I still managed to bat myself into a hole, courtesy of a few plays and misses that rocked my confidence no end. Soon enough I was trapped LBW for 17, well before I got the chance to ask for a second pair of batting gloves. A decent start, I guess, but not nearly enough to get my name in the paper (if they still even do that). On my walk back to the pavilion I'd hoped for at least a couple of claps, some scattered applause to acknowledge my time at the crease, but aside from a 'bad luck' from the opposition scorer, there was nothing. For a fleeting moment I considered throwing my bat at something—mainly to let others know that I was disappointed at getting out—but honestly, I wasn't sure whether I even *was* upset. In fact, I felt nothing but apathy.

At the end of the day's play, I realised the match had really taken it out of me, much more than it used to. It could have been the heat, the fact I was getting older, or the four beers I consumed in the post-match showers, but whatever it was, I couldn't shake the sense that something wasn't quite right. My first game of grade cricket after eighteen months in the wilderness and I felt absolutely nothing whatsoever. Was this evidence of a newfound maturity—an acceptance that cricket is 'just a game'—or a severe case of ennui?

'Was it always like this, Nuggsy?' I asked as we pulled into the bottle shop on our way home. 'Was grade cricket always like this?'

'Mate, don't kid yourself. It's not always this good.'

10

OUTLAW

When I was a kid, I wanted nothing more than to play cricket for Australia. Things like school and homework were only getting in the way of time that could be spent in the nets or the backyard, working on my game, bettering my chances of representing my country as a professional cricketer. Growing up, I'd always longed to work at Queensgrove Sports Centre, arguably the most respected cricket warehouse in the Southern Hemisphere, a one-stop shop for any aspirational cricketer who needed the latest kit. I knew that some of Australia's most famous cricketers had got their first job working the floor at Queensgrove—indeed, the networking opportunities alone made it the perfect part-time gig for a young adult whose sights were firmly set on the big time.

But as we move into adulthood, we find ourselves

naturally moving away from the things we desired as a child. We graduate from school or university and start to figure out our career paths in more detail. What do you want to do with your life? Do you want to have a job that provides you with strong earning potential and/or the ability to transfer your skills overseas, or are you willing to sacrifice salary to do something that you 'love'? Ultimately, there comes a point in one's life when a part-time gig at a sports apparel store is no longer cause for celebration, a stepping stone on your road to international cricket fame, but merely a sad indictment of your 'failure to launch' into adulthood.

With no other form of income, I'd reluctantly taken a casual store attendant position at the multi-sport equipment and apparel chain Outlaw Sport. My job description was basically to facilitate the sale of low-quality cricket bats, footballs, jerseys, tennis racquets, sneakers and activewear. For a fifteen-year-old boy, this job was heaven. For a 31-year-old male, it was depressing. I should also point out that this was a hook-up through Bretty—a career retail specialist, most recently at Big W—who was currently the store manager (and effectively my 'boss').

Bretty was all charm and charisma, a complete natural at retail sales. I'd spent a lot of time alongside Bretty as teammates but never in a professional setting. I wondered whether his recent marriage, let alone becoming a stepfather to four young boys, had resulted in a more mature outlook. Really, very little had changed at all with regards to how Bretty carried himself, both publicly and in one-on-one conversations. The once revered Chop King was lewd and wildly inappropriate by default. That said, I was hoping to leverage Bretty's skill with the ladies into some quick wins of my own (bear in mind that, since Lara, I was yet to get off the mark, so to speak).

With just half an hour until knock off, I was circling around the cricket equipment section as I'd so often done as a youth, only this time I was being paid a gross rate of $19.42 per hour for the privilege of doing so. I busied myself by rearranging a small number of products, silently judging the quality of the Kashmir willow sticks and wishing I was working at Queensgrove, where at least the bats are rarefied premium willow. Over on the other side of the store, Bretty was standing by the gym equipment section, lifting a weighted bar to pump out twenty-five bicep curls with perfect form. I'd always wondered how he managed to have a protruding vein on his bicep at all times and I guess this went some way towards explaining that. It was a small window into his vanity, but fuck he looked good. He always looked good.

As I leant down to pick up a Lonsdale gym singlet that had escaped from its coat hanger, I heard the entrance chime. Our attention turned to the person who had entered the store, a young, blonde female, conventionally attractive by Western standards, who was most likely here to purchase some activewear, or perhaps a set of two-kilo dumbbells.

Bretty walked over to me, disgruntled at a customer coming into the store so near to closing time but equally pleased at the opportunity to make someone fall in love with him.

'Generous seven and a half,' he mumbled.

'What?' I pretended not to know what he was referring to.

'Hockey player. Definitely,' he continued.

'Nah. Netball. Wing attack,' I countered. The specificity of my claim drew a furrowed brow from my manager.

With all the confidence of a man who had never been turned down for anything other than a credit card, Bretty walked over to the customer, strutting like a peacock towards her. His hair-cum-feathers elegantly swayed through the air-conditioned night, the bicep pump from two minutes earlier giving his skin a heavenly glow as his perfect teeth were revealed via his million-dollar smile. He was a God in a black polo and this was his afterlife.

'Hi there!' Bretty opened. 'What can we help you with today?'

The girl clutched an iPhone and navy wallet in one hand; a gold bracelet drooped off the other. Aesthetically speaking, she was no different from many of the dozens of women who came in and out of the store each day—lean, blonde and sporty-looking, decked out in ripped jeans, a white T-shirt and Nike kicks. What was more remarkable, however, was her body language. While most women would already have fallen deep into Bretty's eyes at this point, this particular girl was standing tall, defiant, a hint of a smirk creeping from the corners of her eyes, similar to how a batsman reacts when the opposition goes up for a ridiculous LBW appeal.

'G'day, champ. Where's your cricket section?' the girl retorted.

Hang on. Did Bretty just get champed?

Unable to muster a coherent response for a good three seconds, Bretty finally pointed in my direction.

'Umm, okay. The *big dog* over there will help you out.'

I managed a welcoming smile as the girl walked over to me, with all the swagger and mojo of a second grade top run scorer at awards night.

'Hey, I'm looking for some batting gloves.'

'Gloves are his specialty. He's played in England. As a *pro*,' Bretty called out on his way to the manager's office.

'Is that right?' the girl said, her eyes widening slightly.

'In another life,' I mumbled wistfully, trying to establish an aura of mystique.

'I play first grade for your women's club. I think I've seen you before at training.'

I'd only been to a few sessions since returning to the grade cricket fold, so it was pretty unlikely she'd seen me there. Furthermore, our club didn't even have a women's affiliate team. There weren't many women around the club, full stop. Nathan's mum would turn up every now and then, much to the delight of Nuggsy, who would take this opportunity to flirt with her in front of her embarrassed son. There was also the group of seventy-year-old women who used to conduct tai chi classes in a corner of the oval, but they'd moved on recently after one was struck on the ankle during a fielding drill; our coach, Bozzo, had brutally admonished the elderly Chinese lady for 'not getting something behind it'. But other than that, no women whatsoever—and certainly no women's team.

Anyway, she'd clearly mistaken me for someone else, but did it really matter? An opportunity had presented itself. I decided to leverage my 'professional' cricketing experience to spruik the benefits of having a spare set of batting gloves. Bretty had always instructed me to 'upsell', plus it was a chance to fractionally increase my sales figures for the quarter (I was down forty per cent quarter on quarter).

'But I never seem to bat long enough to need two pairs. Are you sure they're necessary?'

'Absolutely. Left- or right-handed?' I asked, feeling increasingly bullish.

'I'm a lefty.'

Batting left-handed is fucking cheating.

'And what pads and gloves do you have at the moment?'

'I've got a Puma bat and New Balance pads.'

What? Doesn't she want to give others the impression she's sponsored?

Supressing my urge to mouth the word 'yuck', I suggested Puma gloves. We walked over to the gloves section, where a sea of brand-new sparkling kit danced under the artificial lights.

She reached out her left hand as I slid the glove onto her wrist. Our eyes locked.

Stay professional here, bud. Stay focused and close the sale.

As I handed over the right glove, she took it from me, never breaking her gaze. I felt myself blushing slightly.

'I'll get you a stick!' I called back, jogging over to retrieve a shitty sixty-dollar Puma blade.

She received the stick from my hands and took guard before launching into an ungainly cover drive, followed by a (no doubt mistimed) pull shot. Her technique was decidedly yuck, but I still found myself becoming slightly aroused. My two passions—sex and cricket—were being triggered, simultaneously. I began to understand why Nuggsy had that life-size poster of Mark Waugh above his bed.

'How do they feel?'

'A bit *stiff*, but that's never a bad thing,' she winked.

The innuendo was not lost on me. Until now, I had considered these types of mildly sexual references the sole reserve of middle-aged heterosexual men. Aside from club dressing-rooms and 'sportsman's lunches', I'd never heard anyone make a cricket-related double entendre—let alone an attractive woman.

'Yeah, you'll just need to wear them in a bit.'

We were joking, flirting, in a room surrounded by discounted sports paraphernalia. This was exhilarating. She put the bat down for a moment.

'What's a guy like you doing in a place like this?' she asked.

We weren't talking about cricket anymore.

'Oh, it's just a stop-gap for now, really. I'm stealing practice balls to sell to my housemate.'

'Hey, do you guys put on grips? I've been going *bareback* the past few weeks and my parents are beginning to worry.'

She was starting to make jokes that I hadn't even heard before. How crude *was* women's cricket? I shuddered at the thought.

'Yeah, we can do that for you. No extra charge.'

'Let me just run to my car and get my bat. Will you stay open for me? I'll just be two minutes.'

'Yeah, no worries.'

At that moment, Bretty came back out from the

manager's office, inexplicably shirtless. I can only guess what he was doing back there.

'Mate, how good.'

I don't even know what that meant, but I went with it.

'Did you get digits?'

'She's coming back, mate. I've just got to regrip her bat.'

'Sweet, I'll pack up the store. Do you want some aftershave?'

Bretty handed me Hugo Boss cologne, the bottle half-empty.

'I'm all good, thanks, Bretty,' I replied somewhat incredulously.

'Suit yourself.'

As he walked back to the office, he sprayed himself four times around the neck and chest before opening up the front of his trousers and executing a fifth spray onto his genitals. It was a weird thing for him to do, considering he was going to a parent-teacher interview directly after his shift.

Soon enough, she walked back into the store, cricket bat in hand.

'I'm Emma, by the way.'

'Nice to meet you. I'm—'

'I can read your name tag.'

The name Emma had instantly sparked a fond memory. A few weeks into our relationship, Lara had introduced me to the folk band Bon Iver, by way of their debut album *For Emma, Forever Ago*. She told me that the singer-songwriter, Justin Vernon, had written the entire album in the solitude of a hunting cabin in Wisconsin, fresh from a devastating break-up. Each lyric dripping with pathos, Vernon's falsetto captured the brutal heartache of love lost—while managing to bring Lara and me together. As you might expect, my appreciation for sensitive indie rock would remain a secret, for I could never tell any of my teammates that I was into this genre of music. This was much the same for many of my extracurricular pursuits, which included a monthly book club and a couples' cooking class. But with Lara now out of the picture, I no longer had any hobbies. I didn't listen to music or go to live gigs. With the exception of the weekly MyCricket results, I'd stopped reading entirely. And it had been months since I'd cooked a meal for myself.

Yes, Lara was good for me.

But *sex* was also good for me, and it was something I hadn't had in a long time. Random, meaningless sex—the kind Bretty used to have in spades—was on the cards here, seemingly for the taking. Would I remember what to do? I was always a nervous starter.

Luckily, Bretty re-emerged to jolt me from these oscillating thoughts, work bag in one hand and store keys in the other. With five minutes left in the shift, the store was still technically open, with the closing and till-counting likely to take another hour or so. But tonight, Bretty had a bigger, more important role to play. Tonight, he wasn't a store manager of a national sports chain. Tonight, he was a wingman.

'You right to lock up tonight, mate?' he shouted, flinging the bundle of keys in my direction without warning.

This was a huge moment. Should I drop them, my credibility as 'the cricketer' in the eyes of Emma would be damaged beyond repair. But I couldn't merely catch the keys. Whether it's a pen thrown from a colleague, a bottle cap flicked by a mate, or a newborn baby passed from a relative, it's not just about being able to catch the thing. It's about doing it as nonchalantly as possible. In order to exhibit a *laissez-faire* approach, I had to channel my inner Mark Waugh. With fingers pointed up, the keys rocketed straight into the middle of my right palm. My decision to keep the left hand in my pocket added to the display of showmanship. Any onlooker would have commented that it looked like I had *time*, as if the entire sequence was in slow motion. There's a reason that Bretty was the career leader in assisted run-outs for the club, for his throw was equally perfect in its precision.

'Nice grab!' Emma exclaimed.

'He doesn't drop 'em! See you tomorrow, *big dog*,' Bretty cried out, before flinging an arm in the air and trotting out of the door.

The store was now completely empty but for Emma and me.

'So, what sort of grip do you want?'

'Ribbed,' Emma said bluntly.

What the fuck is a ribbed batting grip?

I plucked a white grip from a box. It had taken me a while, but with Bretty gone, I was now warming to the idea of this role-play scenario.

'I can't believe you've been batting without a grip. I usually put two on. Feels thicker in my hands,' I quipped.

'Safety first!' she whispered seductively.

I placed Emma's bat between my legs, the handle protruding upward from my thighs, before hunching over to place the batting cone over the handle, gradually rolling the grip down towards the handle shaft. To my horror, the batting cone jolted out of my hands and onto the floor before the grip had transferred fully onto the handle. Performance anxiety had struck at the worst possible time.

'Nervous?' she said. 'Here, let me help you.'

Her bat was still between my legs. She calmly repositioned the cone over the handle and rolled the grip all the way to the base. It was clear this wasn't the first time she'd applied a new handle to a cricket bat.

'You're about to get off, aren't you?' she whispered.

What?

'I mean, it's 8 p.m . . .'

'Ah, well, yeah, I've just got to close up shop. Do you still want to buy this stuff?'

Emma leaned in, breathing in my second-hand cologne for just a moment.

'Forget the second pair of gloves. Let's have a drink at yours? I don't mind playing an away game,' she purred.

I woke up the next morning, sheets a tangled mess, and reached over to the other side of the bed, only to realise that Emma wasn't there. Somewhat surprised, I gauged she'd made her way out to put on some coffee while waiting for me to arise, much like Lara used to on Sunday mornings.

The moment I opened the door I saw Bruiser and Nuggsy standing there in the kitchen. They turned to me and started applauding.

'Here's the big man!'

'You salty old dog! You *sailor*, you!'

'Verified *chop*! Huge!'

I'd walked out of my bedroom to be greeted by a series of backslaps and handshakes. At that moment, Nathan walked in through the door.

'What's going on here?'

'Old mate got a *chop* last night!' Nuggsy bellowed, again slapping me on the back.

'Huge if true!' Nathan cried, eyes darting around to ensure he'd used the appropriate lexicon.

'Mate, not only is it *true*, but Bruiser and I met her this morning!' continued Nuggsy.

Oh, shit.

'And get this . . .'

Fuck, where is this going?

'Absolute fucking pisser . . .' Bruiser cut in, barely able to hide his laughter. Nuggsy was attempting to conceal his own giggles, only to let out a crass snort. Meanwhile, Nathan's eyes lit up in anticipation.

'. . . She walked out of his room in *full fucking whites!*'

The three of them collapsed into hysterics as I stood there, in the centre of the room, in nothing but my silk boxers. I'd expected to come out and have a quick piece of toast with Emma before ordering her an Uber and making plans to catch up again soon, but instead, my friends were subjecting me to public humiliation. I wondered if Emma had at least kissed me on the cheek before leaving, but that seemed increasingly unlikely.

Bruiser took a breath to compose himself.

'Mate, to be fair, she is a *sweetheart*.'

He clutched both hands together to his chest, intertwining his fingers with a complete lack of sincerity.

'Yeah, credit where credit's due. She's an absolute nine out of ten,' Nuggsy offered.

'Generous nine and a half, even!' Bruiser said over the top.

It was nice to know that my mates approved of the woman I had slept with, even going so far as to award her a generous rating out of ten. However, I couldn't help but feel that something about this was wrong. The chop itself had come a little too easily, in retrospect. I backed into my room as the celebration of my sexual conquest continued to echo through the apartment walls.

I checked my phone, only to be greeted by zero notifications. I whipped together a quick text to Emma: *Nice to meet you, hope to catch up soon.* I pressed send.

Message failed to send.

I resent the message.

Message failed to send.

Confused, I frantically checked Emma's number in my phone contacts.

123456$#(.

I decided to give her the benefit of the doubt. We'd had a few drinks at my place, but I didn't think she'd be the kind of person to enter a fake number into my phone. It must have been an error. I remembered that her last name was Michaels, which served to calm my nerves. All was not lost: I could just look her up on MyCricket.

Then it dawned on me. Over the other side of the

room, I noticed a gaping hole on my chest of drawers. My under-11 hat-trick ball was missing. The ball had been mounted on a small wooden plank. On that base was a gold-coloured plate, upon which my name and bowling figures had been engraved. This memento symbolised everything that was great in my life: it was all of the hope that I had then and whatever ounce of hope I had left, both on and off the field. Even twenty years on, the seam was still proud and pronounced. Every time I looked at it I was taken back to that wonderful summer's afternoon among childhood friends.

And now, it had been stolen.

A horrifying realisation suddenly dawned on me. My old teammate Damo used to steal things from his Friday night sexual conquests and show them to us during the stretching circle on Saturday. He started with something simple, say, a remote control or a toothbrush, but gradually moved on to taking treasured personal items, like a family photo, or a diary. I'd even done this once, back when I played a season in the UK. After a boozy night out I'd stolen a girl's remote control and brandished it to the lads in order to assert myself as the alpha dog. By stealing someone's personal items after sex, not only are you saying 'I managed to have sex last night' but also 'I am comfortable humiliating this person who I barely know behind her back'. Sure, this is all excusable behaviour that falls under the subject of 'banter', but I'd always felt guilty for sinking to Damo's level. And now, Emma had taken something from me that I held very dearly. This was well beyond the pale in terms of being a bit of light-hearted fun. I mean, sure, if you take a TV remote, it's annoying as fuck to watch TV, but you can usually still operate the thing. But this was like stealing someone's heart medication. I fucking needed that hat-trick ball.

I couldn't help but picture Emma holding court in the stretching circle before her game, describing the way she'd cunningly seduced this desperate, lonely grade cricketer into a sexual tryst. With all ten teammates huddled around her, she'd go into graphic detail of my ungainly body shape before mocking my birthmark and the size of my calves, revealing all my shortcomings to a pack of hungry lionesses. She'd mimic the faces I pulled right towards the end, just before I told her that I loved her. Then, and only then, would she reveal my hat-trick ball to the team. She'd hold it dramatically above her head, like Simba being revealed to the herd on Pride Rock, showing it off as the cheap and insignificant accomplishment that it was. Backslaps all around. The team would then break for a fielding drill, fully energised and raring to go off the back of a raucous chop story. The perfect way to kick off a Saturday morning of cricket.

Yep, this is what it feels like to get fucked by the Chop King.

11

THIRTEENTH MAN

In order to play cricket for Australia, one must first make it through the challenging grade cricket system. And that's pretty much the one thing that keeps grade cricket in the conversation today: the fact that it is simply unavoidable.

No matter how talented you are, whether you're Steve Smith or Don Bradman, you can't just bypass grade cricket on your journey to the top. In that sense, grade cricket is a bit like airport security: it's a fucking ball-ache, sure, but you're not going to board that plane until you step through a metal detector and let some faceless security automaton open up your carry-on baggage to remove a tube of moisturiser because you're twenty millilitres over the limit. Every young kid who comes through grade cricket these days is subject to this same invasive treatment, and whether he prospers or flounders will depend on how quickly he gets the fuck out of there. For the longer you spend in grade cricket, the less likely you are to 'make it'. If Bradman didn't fluke a ton on debut, chances are he would have spent the next fifteen to twenty years floating between second and third grade, juggling grade cricket commitments with a part-time job working at a sports apparel store or call centre. Some are able to swiftly rise through the ranks to reach the professional level while the rest of us languish in the cesspool of despair and disappointment that is grade cricket.

Nuggsy was good mates with our state player, Dessie Harrington. Dessie and Nuggsy had played juniors together—Nuggsy a bustling fast medium bowler, Dessie an elegant top-order batsman—yet they'd paved remarkably divergent paths: one had gone on to play professional cricket for his state, the other had been secretly fixing grade cricket matches in order to pay off significant gambling debts. I still remember when Dessie burst onto the scene as a precocious sixteen-year-old, well over a decade ago, quickly earning a state call-up at the age of nineteen, bound for higher honours. As a young player of promise, I viewed Dessie's swift ascent as hard evidence that a kid like me could make it.

Even though Dessie was a state-contracted player, he still made the effort to turn up to grade cricket training every now and then, even when he wasn't playing. It wasn't just a token gesture either. While most state players will spend their time at the side of the nets, arms crossed and full state kit on, talking to the club president while staring vacantly ahead, Dessie was an active participant. He'd even stick around and run the whole-of-club fielding drills, drawing on his professional experience to enhance the skills of those around him. He was the exact opposite of Lawro, the first state player I came across in my debut season of grade cricket, who once asked me to feed him a ball machine for three hours straight (4.30 to 7.30 p.m.). Throughout the entire session, never once did he make eye contact with me. To him I was merely an extension of the ball machine itself, a critical yet faceless cog in the industrial production process. Personally, I look forward to the onset of a fully automated society, one where ball machines are able to feed themselves, so that future generations will never be subjected to the same degrading experience that I was as a young man. While they're at it, perhaps they can invent a batting machine as well, so we don't have to play this fucking sport anymore.

Anyway, I'd gotten to know Dessie through Nuggsy over the past couple of months. He'd come over to our place one evening after training, where we binned more than a few beers and started talking about life after cricket. He waited patiently for me to finish my thirty-minute diatribe on the lack of support systems available for retiring grade cricketers before opening up on his 'fear of the unknown'. Dessie was once described by a prominent News Corp journalist as 'the next Mark Waugh', but that was way back in the early 2000s, when every vaguely stylish right-hand batsman with the ability to clip one forward of square leg was heralded as such. Alas, Dessie was more like the cricketing equivalent of a busted IPO: his initial stock price surged upon breaking into the state side, whereupon he mustered a few daddy 50s in quick succession, but his market price dived after a couple of failures and he never managed to recapture that buzz. Indeed, over the past decade or so, Dessie had floated on the periphery of the state squad. A bit of T20 cricket, a few one dayers, three or four Shield matches a season, but never enough to truly cement himself. Barring an unexpected late renaissance, Dessie's career had already well and truly peaked. He was still a contracted player, probably on about eighty or ninety grand, but with bills mounting up and a kid on the way, he was starting to think about the next stage of his life. For athletes, once the thinking starts, it's as good as over.

The thing about cricket is that it demands everything of you and gives very little in return. Over the years, I've known very few players who've managed to forge a successful professional career while playing grade cricket, regardless of the level. Whenever I was cc'd on a whole-of-club email about an upcoming raffle, barbecue or whatever, I'd scan the list of recipients just to see if any of my clubmates had a job. Occasionally there'd be one or two there, b.mathison@pwc.com.au or damianjohnston@visa.org sitting incongruously among the crude Hotmail, Gmail and AOL accounts, most ending with the number '69'. My old teammate Donny continues to have Big_Dick_Donny6969@hotmail.com as his primary channel of communication; he's thirty-five and married with three kids but still uses the email address he came up with as a fifteen-year-old. To succeed in grade cricket (and by 'succeed' I mean play first or second grade to reasonable acclaim), it's actually more advantageous to be completely unemployed. For starters, you don't have to make up a bullshit excuse to leave work early on Tuesdays and Thursdays for training. Those of us with jobs have to sneak out at 4.30 p.m. and fight peak-hour traffic just to get a hit before the sun goes down. Without the burden of a job, you can dedicate all your mental energy to achieving your ultimate dream: a T20 Big Bash contract, eight to ten thousand new Twitter followers, two or three months of blissful financial security, and state cricket apparel.

I was able to see the human side of a professional cricketer for the first time. They weren't invincible; they too have hopes and dreams, fears and anxieties, mortgages and bills. They are just like us, only with better skinfold percentages, natural athleticism, and sporting ability the rest of us can only dream of possessing.

Still, imagine being a professional cricketer ...

Another Saturday, another grim grade cricket experience. Second day of a two dayer—1-8 overnight chasing 3-352 (declared). The suffocating familiarity of it all. I could already see how this one would pan out. We'd start slowly, crawling along at one an over for the first ten before the wickets start tumbling. One would bring two, then three, soon six. A range of familiar emotions would be felt over the course of a few hours: denial, anger, bargaining, depression. Basically, every Saturday followed the Kübler-Ross model (also known as the five stages of grief), only without the 'acceptance' at the end.

With ten minutes left until the start of play, I felt my phone vibrate in my kit. To my surprise, it was Dessie.

'Hi, mate,' I answered. 'Aren't you playing today?'

'Nah, mate. I'm fucking twelfth man again. They've asked me to go back to grade to have a hit because ones are batting.'

'Ah, fuck.'

'Threes are fielding, right?'

'Yeah, that's right.'

'Well, they need me to find someone to fill in as the sub. You want in?'

I gulped, unsure of whether this was a stitch-up. I knew that this was a 'thing', in that state selectors often encourage the twelfth man to go back to grade cricket and find a bit of form rather than sit around all day running the drinks. In these types of situations, the twelfth man is asked to call up someone from his grade club to take over these admin-istrative responsibilities and act as a sub-fielder if required. So Dessie had chosen to contact me, a 31-year-old third grader with hands like glass, to take his place.

Even though I knew where he was going with this, I needed him to say the actual words.

'What do you mean, mate?'

'Come and be the twelfth man today. That way I can have a stick in ones. We'd need you to get over here pretty sharp, though.'

I hesitated, bound by shock. Eventually I responded.

'But I'm in third grade—don't they want someone from twos at least?'

'Nah, they don't care, mate. You should have seen the bloke we had for our last game. Absolute pisser. Bloke could barely run in a straight line. Anyway, you said you wanted to know what it's like to be a professional cricketer for a day, right? Here's your chance.'

I clutched the phone to my chest and looked around at my teammates. Could I leave them high and dry? Fuck, would anyone even *notice* I'd gone? What sense of duty did I have to these blokes, anyway? I barely knew any of these kids. They certainly didn't know me. In truth, I'd felt out of place upon my return to grade cricket. Not young enough to be a contemporary, not old enough to carry the gravitas of a 'father figure'. Meanwhile, Nuggsy was sitting right next to me, completely oblivious to the conversation I was having. His focus was firmly on the grotesque sausage roll he'd purchased that morning from the 7-Eleven—one of those king-size ones that truck drivers tend to favour—which he had chosen to pair with a 600-millilitre iced coffee–flavoured Dare. To complete the vision of ill health, a slim Peter Stuyvesant cigarette dangled between the middle and ring fingers on his right hand (the one holding the Dare), its embers quickly burning towards the filter.

I grabbed the car keys out of Nuggsy's kit bag.

'Just running to the car, mate,' I explained. 'I think I left my zinc in the boot.'

'All good,' he replied, crumbs flying out of his mouth.

I hopped in the car and left the ground without looking back.

A million thoughts raced through my head as I stood at the door to the dressing-room. An elderly man named Neville, whom I took to be some form of unpaid official, had escorted me from the car park to the dressing-room. He appeared to know every inch of this historic sports complex, arguably Australia's most celebrated sporting venue. Neville, who walked at a fair clip for a bloke in his eighties, had whisked me through the bowels of the stadium, as if we were Viet Cong soldiers making our way through secret man-made tunnels to launch a surprise attack on the enemy. Finally, we emerged up a stairwell and through a secret door into the main hall. I breathed in the surroundings. All around me were photographs and memorabilia celebrating the cricketing legends who had graced this ground. From Bradman to Trumper, McCabe, Hassett, Benaud, and into the modern day. All of them. And now, me. It hit me that I would be playing a game of cricket at the same ground that Bradman scored a test hundred on.

Stand tall. Focus on your posture. Firm handshake. Solid eye contact. You've got this, mate.

Neville stood in the middle of the room, cleared his throat, and announced in a thin, quavering voice that I would be replacing Dessie as twelfth man for the day. I stood there proudly, waiting for a reaction, but no one was even listening. Graham Deakin, the veteran wicketkeeper, was describing his wife's reaction to a fart he had performed in bed the previous evening.

'It was so bloody filthy that it woke her up!' he roared to howls of laughter.

A few moments passed as the team composed themselves, before 'Deeks' noticed me standing there in the middle of the room.

'Hang on, are you from the Make-A-Wish Foundation or something?'

I found it baffling that he would immediately assume the only reason I was here in the dressing-room was for a charitable organisation that aims to grant experience-based 'wishes' to young people battling terminal illnesses.

'No, this is our twelfth man for today, boys. Make him welcome.'

From the corner of my eye I noticed a shadowy figure emerging out of the showers. I pivoted my body to face him directly as the room fell silent. He was tall, six-three-ish, bald and completely naked. I instantly recognised this was Michael 'Mad Dog' McDougall, the former test opening bowler and leading wicket taker in this season's Sheffield Shield. He walked straight over to me with purpose, a mischievous grin on his face, before wrapping his right hand around his penis and slowly yet rhythmically pulling it from base to head.

'Who are you?' he grinned, putting his hand out to greet me.

With no option, I feebly took his hand in mine. Again, the room broke out in laughter, but at least the ice was broken. And at least they had noticed me. Someone walked behind me and ruffled my hair. It felt good, perhaps a little too good. I was one of the boys now. Shaking Mad Dog's hand immediately post penis-stroke was a small price to pay for begrudging inclusion and acceptance.

I had expected the warm-up to be full-on but it was actually a rather relaxed (if highly skilled) affair. Many of the players spent considerable time chatting to the opposition players. There was none of the intensity we experience in lower grade cricket, where a humble T drill is performed as if it were a military exercise. It made sense—for them, this was *work*. It was highly compartmentalised: a couple of blokes in a slips cordon, a few others on sharp ground fielding drills, a few other blokes rolling their arm over at a stump with keeper in tow. With the warm-up done, we all filed back into the dressing-rooms to get into our whites. I had been issued a pair of creams and a state shirt, which I was sternly instructed to return at the close of play (a little too forcefully if you ask me).

As everyone was undertaking their last-minute preparations, Mad Dog thought it would be an opportune time to run a straw poll of the number of people in the team who would be willing to perform cunnilingus on a sex worker (although he definitely did not use the word *cunnilingus* but rather a far more uncouth phrase that I hadn't even heard of until that day yet cannot ever erase from my memory). As you might imagine, this had the effect of deeply dividing the group: some, including the older, bookish types, simply walked out of the room in disgust; others were only too willing to share their deviant tendencies in graphic detail. It wasn't as if Mad Dog was having this conversation off to one side—it was as if he were Tony Jones on ABC's *Q&A*, moderating a discussion about same-sex marriage, striving to give both sides a chance to respond. I don't think he even realised that there was a grade cricketer in the room who had seen him play for Australia (and appear in several advertisements as a brand ambassador for a prominent multivitamins company), but there I was in the corner of the room, in awe, silently soaking it all in.

Just as Mad Dog's panel discussion drew to a close, the coach walked into the room. He was a former state cricketer, highly regarded for his tactical thinking, recently mooted as a possible successor to the current Australian coach. Holding an open MacBook in his hand, he listened and nodded intently as the skipper gave his pre-match address.

'Alright, lads, let's have a big session out there.'

Perhaps it was the sensation of being in a professional dressing-room but I couldn't help myself.

'Work *hard*, lads!'

Once again, the entire room fell deathly silent. The whole playing group turned around to look at me as if I'd just dropped an insensitive racial comment. In some ways it was worse than outing myself as a racist. I'd just announced myself as a grade cricketer. Or even worse, a park cricketer.

'Work *hard*? That's fucking *grade* cricket chat, champ,' the skipper chortled mirthlessly.

'Who are you again?' someone else chirped.

Third time someone's asked that.

As the team began to file out, the other opening bowler—a long-haired, left-arm quick who'd played a little bit of international cricket here and there—came up to me and shoved a circular container of lip balm into my hand.

'Run this out to me every five overs. I don't want to field with it in my pocket.'

'Sure, no worries.'

'Thanks, champ.'

Whether it's the sly 'what can I get you, *champ*' from a barista, or a 'did you tap on there, *pal*' from an eagled-eyed bus driver, life in itself is a constant alpha showdown. These days I can barely communicate with another human being—male *or* female—without wondering whether I'm being belittled in some form or another. In this case there was no need for such contemplation, as it was abundantly clear I was indeed being belittled. Of course, I know and accept that blokes have been alpha-ing each other forever. In Shakespeare's *Taming of the Shrew*, Curtis exclaims to the diminutive Grumio during a heated exchange: 'Away, you three-inch fool! I am no beast!' If Curtis had a crack like that today at Grumio's manhood he'd almost certainly be the victim of a one-punch attack. Especially if Grumio had already smashed twelve schooners and a couple of MDMA caps.

Anyway, this trend was to continue throughout the day—I'd be summoned onto the field to perform menial tasks for the playing group. At one point the captain called me onto the ground to tell me he'd forgotten to put a ticket on the gate for a friend, and asked me to speak to the gate-keeper to organise one. Another player asked me to call his wife and tell her to put three hundred on a horse in Race 3 at Randwick. The coach himself even asked me to pop across the road and pick up his dry-cleaning. I was only too happy to take care of their admin.

For the rest of the day, I watched the match unfold from the players' area. Being a 'player' afforded me instant status. Saturday was Kids Day, and there were young children running around everywhere with miniature cricket bats in tow. If these kids weren't there I reckon there would have been about eight paid spectators in attendance, so they were at least able to create the illusion that this was a professional match of some significance.

As I sat in the players' area with my feet on the railing, I noticed a mother lurking below with her son. They were waving up at me, trying to get my attention for some reason. I moved over to peer over the pavilion.

'Hi, how can I help?'

'Can you sign my boy's bat?' she asked politely. It didn't escape me that she was quite an attractive woman, perhaps in her early thirties.

'I'm actually just filling in for the day,' I called back, immediately regretting my honesty. I would have loved to sign that kid's bat.

'That's okay—just sign it anyway,' she replied with a smile.

I looked over to see what the coach was up to. He was just staring at his fucking laptop, as always.

As a boy, I had honed my signature in the hope that one day I'd be asked to autograph a mini-bat. Finally, that day had arrived. The kid passed his bat over the fence and I signed it. On cue, about forty or fifty more kids came running over, having realised that a professional cricketer was dishing out autographs. Twenty minutes later I had devalued everyone's merchandise. Every bat was signed in the correct manner: a cold request for the child's name, a half-cocked smile, and eyes directed over the child's shoulder when finally presenting them with the auto-graph. Zero eye contact was critical.

Eventually, the opening bowler—not Mad Dog, but the bloke who'd asked me to run his lip balm out every five overs—had to go off for an injury check. Quite embarrassingly, he'd rolled his ankle fielding a ball that was gently padded back to him off his own bowling.

Finally, my moment had arrived.

'Get your spikes on, pal,' the coach yelled.

I sprinted into the dressing-room and reached into my kit to pull out my cricket boots. I'd slipped them off with the laces still done up after the warm-up, which made it hard to put them back on. I tried to undo the knot by yanking one string, but this had the effect of creating an even more complicated knot, which I had no idea how to resolve. It was just like my old dream of getting timed out, only on a grander scale.

'Hurry up!' the coach blared.

'Coming!' I yelled back. I gritted my teeth and forced both shoes on, and made my way out of the sheds. A couple of kids clapped as I sprinted down the tunnel onto the hallowed turf. I could overhear one of them say to the other, 'Who is that guy?' It was a fair question.

'Fine leg, champion,' the skipper yelled, his voice echoing around the largely vacant arena. The acoustics were tremendous; I could hear everything.

For the next five or six overs, I performed a fine leg to deep mid-off rotation. There I was, isolated and alone, praying that the ball wouldn't come my way. The first time I touched the ball was when I was moved up into the conventional mid-off position. Mad Dog bowled a half-volley, which was crunched down the ground by their opening batsman, a stocky left-hander who had recently been dropped from the test side. He hit it with such force that I barely had time to get down to it. Next ball he worked a single down to fine leg and eyeballed me the whole way down the pitch. Throughout the entire over he continued to stare at me between balls, clearly trying to work how who the fuck I was. Maybe he thought I was from the Make-A-Wish Foundation too. I noticed that the next ball he hit my way came with far less venom.

A couple of overs later and I was called into action. The right-handed opener had skipped down the wicket, looking for quick runs, and launched our spinner down to deep mid-off. I saw it early and moved well as it sailed slightly to my left. Normally, I'd be squinting into the sun, but the 360-degree stadium had factored that out of the equation. The imaginary crowd roared in the background, but I kept my composure amid the pressure. I put my hands out with my fingers proudly up (the patented Australian way of catching a cricket ball) and held my breath.

It stuck, like glue.

Some scattered applause emanated from the members' part of the stadium. Perhaps six pairs of hands, maybe seven, but to me it felt like I'd just taken a Schweppes Classic Catch in front of a packed Bay 13 in 1992/93. I had expected to be wholly embraced by my new teammates, to fall into their arms—perhaps even be hoisted onto someone's shoulders—but no one walked towards me. In fact, I had to sprint a full eighty metres to join the celebration circle, which had all the energy of a wake. The opposition was around 2-300, so 'we' were no chance of bowling them out before the end of the day. We had congregated together because that's what people do when they get a wicket, they go and stand next to each other. Given the exposure these athletes would have had to various high-performance coaches over the years, I expected a few motivational phrases to be trotted out at the very least. But there was nothing—well, not until Mad Dog broke the silence with what had become the common refrain of the day.

'So, who are you?'

I felt the sudden urge to explain who I was, where I'd come from, how I knew Dessie, what I was even *doing* here, but just as I was about to provide all that contextual information, the umpire called us into position and I was left to walk back down to deep mid-off without so much as a pat on the back.

Alone, again.

I looked over at the electronic scoreboard to see my name in lights, but the dismissal just read 'caught (sub)'. Who was I, indeed? I felt like one of those seat-fillers at the Oscars, just plugging the gaps while some Oscar-nominated actor ducks off to the bathroom to do a line of coke. Another couple of overs passed before I was summoned from the field, replaced by the injury-prone fast bowler. I had performed my duties to the required standard but now it was time for me to get the fuck off the field.

'Don't forget to run my lip balm out every five overs,' he thundered as he ran past.

I made my way into the dressing-room to change out of my spikes. The coach ambled in, MacBook in his left hand. I could see an unfinished game of Solitaire on the screen.

'You can leave now. Dessie's on his way back,' he mumbled. 'Take your whites off and leave them on the ground—Neville will wash 'em for us.'

'Thanks, coach.'

'Who are you again?' he asked, this time with a smile on his face, conscious that this sentence had become a running joke.

I began to answer, but he started shuffling out of the room the moment my mouth opened.

And just like that, my brief dalliance with the professional arena was over as quickly as it had arrived.

Hang on, I can't leave without nicking some kit.

I looked around the room. I realised I had about one minute to make hay before being accused of lingering. Should I nick someone's second pair of gloves? A bat? Someone's state lid? Some Bradman memorabilia off the wall?

Before I could act on any of these impulses, some new bloke with a lanyard came in to hasten my departure.

'Come on, mate, off we go.'

So, off I went, with nothing to show for my day other than a half-used tub of Blistex in my pocket.

12

LE VÉRITABLE
NUGGSY

'You ready, mate?' I yelled from outside Nuggsy's bedroom. 'We're going to be late otherwise.'

Nuggsy's typical pre-circuit routine involved grabbing a dirty V-neck T-shirt from the laundry basket and spraying 500 millilitres of Lynx Africa on all parts of his body—including his genital region, just in case some lucky lady chose to 'explore the Nuggler' later that evening—and he was good to go. Being completely bald—not a skerrick of hair remained on his head these days—was a real time-saver, in that there was no need for a blow dryer or a hair straightener (one of Nathan's favourite appliances) to get an unruly salad in order. But tonight, he'd been in there for a good hour or so, far longer than he usually spent preparing for an evening out.

When Nuggsy finally emerged from the en suite, it was

immediately evident that this would be no ordinary night out. Gone was the dirty V-neck with fictitious Mexican beach resort town and arbitrary number emblazoned on the front (Costa de la Playa 1978) and in its place a white tuxedo shirt with French-cut sleeves, a stylish midnight-blue jacket slung over his shoulder. Nuggsy had transformed his aesthetic from Big Day Out pill popper to *GQ* model in the space of forty-five minutes. He walked over to the hall mirror and began toying with a bow tie—not a clip-on, but a proper bow tie with ribbons and shit.

He still hadn't said a word.

'Didn't realise this was a black-tie event,' I joked.

Nuggsy looked me and my Tarocash shirt up and down. I braced for the inevitable insult, but it never came.

'You ever learn how to tie a bow tie?' he asked jovially.

'Umm, no, Nuggsy.'

Nuggsy smiled at me in the mirror's reflection, sensing an opportunity to assume his natural role of *senpai*.

'Well, mate, you start with the tie facing up. You don't want to fuck that up. Then make sure one side—the right side, in this instance—is shorter than the left.'

He dexterously moved the right side across and under the left-hand side of the tie and up through the loop of the neck.

'You see this joint here? Well, now you've gotta fold this bit towards the right, then over to the left to create the bow shape. Then bring this bit over the middle, fold this fucker over that way and pinch the fold.'

I wasn't sure what was more impressive: Nuggsy's bow-tying ability itself or the fact he'd managed to turn a bow-tying tutorial into yet another display of dominance.

'Then just push the pinched bit through the loop behind here, pull the folded bit to tighten her up, and then we just balance it out on both sides . . . and *voilà!*'

It hadn't escaped me how perfectly he had pronounced the French word *voilà*.

We'd played cricket earlier that day—snuck home in a thriller—and normally that would have been cause for some serious celebration. Nuggsy had taken 3-17 in a dynamic four-over spell, which had effectively tipped the game in our favour. I'd chipped in with a valuable 30-odd (23) at number six as we chased down their total of 164 with just two wickets to spare. But looking around the sheds at the conclusion of the game, I hardly recognised the faces. Ten minutes later, the dressing-room was already empty. Our young teammates had no interest in sticking around for a shower and a few beers. As Nuggsy and I took our post-match shower, beer in one hand, soap in the other, teammates already long departed, I realised that things would never be the same again.

All our mates from years gone by had stopped playing cricket. Dazza, Robbo, Haynesy. Deeks, Bretty, Chooka. They'd all retired for different reasons—some through injury, others due to family commitments. Haynesy had taken a job interstate and was firmly focusing on building his career. Chooka, who'd recently turned forty, had to take his young teenage children to *their* Saturday matches. Meanwhile, Deeks had been put on the sex offenders list, which meant he wasn't allowed within two hundred metres of a school, thus preventing him from attending training (the home ground was directly next to a Catholic girls' college).

Blokes like Chooka, Ducko, Rooster and Goose had been replaced by youngsters like Aaron, Stephane, Hudson and Kai. And these new blokes would never be given affectionate poultry-based nicknames.

It was Nuggsy's thirty-seventh birthday, an occasion that would usually be marked out on the circuit. However, in a strange break from tradition, I had been informed at late notice that tonight we would be dining with his parents instead. Here I must point out that, despite knowing Nuggsy for over a decade, I'd never actually met his parents. In fact, Nuggsy's entire upbringing was a mystery to me. Aside from him being a junior cricket prodigy, swiftly elevated to the upper echelons of grade cricket before his eighteenth birthday—all this is on the public record—there was very little interpersonal information for me to go on. Unlike me—and, indeed, many others I've played with—Nuggsy had no deep-seated desire to seek his father's validation through cricket. I'd never seen Nuggsy's dad come to any games. Not once. In the whole time I'd known him, he'd never even *mentioned* his parents, which led me to wonder how Nuggsy had come to be the person he was today. Was it nature, nurture, or a combination of the two that had produced the likes of Alan Nugget?

I'd always just assumed that Nuggsy had a tough upbringing, which is partly why I looked sympathetically upon his various vices. I'd constructed my own narrative: Alan Nugget's father, 'Ray', was a large, bald man in his fifties, with a far-too aggressive handshake and a debilitating gambling addiction, who stank of stale cigarettes and bad credit. His mother, 'Cheryl', who had suffered from a decades-long meth addiction, gave birth to the young Alan at the tender age of sixteen. Nuggsy's parents were on government benefits, living in estate housing in a low socio-economic area, probably somewhere out past the airport. It was an unhappy childhood marred by alcohol-fuelled domestic violence. Eventually, the Department of Community Services was forced to intervene, and Nuggsy was put into foster care, where he lived with a gentle couple in their sixties who'd been unable to have children of their own. Ultimately, he rebelled against their middle-class suburban lifestyle and found solace in grade cricket—his true 'family'. It had all the makings of a wrong-side-of-the-tracks Hollywood movie.

I'd expected the Uber driver to take us in the general direction of the airport, but forty-five minutes later I found myself on the doorstep of a three-storey mansion in a leafy part of town. Nuggsy rang the doorbell once and stood back, allowing the chime to ring out, as footsteps approached. A few moments passed before a slender man with a full head of medium-length silver hair and a soft European tan opened the door. He was dressed in a baby-blue cardigan, fitted chinos and white loafers, as if plucked straight from a dating website for women over fifty.

'Hello, gentlemen,' he announced, in what I instantly gauged to be a French accent, before turning to face Nuggsy directly.

'Alain, come here and give your papa a hug.'

'Come on, Dad,' Nuggsy replied, before reluctantly leaning forward for a lengthy physical embrace that most Australian men would find horrifying.

Papa? Alain?

Mr Nugget smiled before turning to me and offering a low-to-medium-strength handshake, the kind you might offer to a woman at a post-conference networking event. His hands were smooth as butter, definitely not the hands of a blue-collar worker.

'Hello, Mr Nugget,' I managed.

I was now pretty confident that my foster parent story was true. Nuggsy's biological parents were either deceased or incarcerated.

'Well, it's actually pronounced *Nugét* but, please, call me Jean-Luc,' he replied convivially. 'Please, come in.'

Nuggsy trailed behind me coyly.

Alain? Nugét? Wait, Nuggsy's real name is Alain Nugét?

There was so much to compute, already. As we walked down the long, carpeted hallway into the dining room, I noticed a woman enter the room from the kitchen.

'*Alain, viens faire un bisou à ta maman!*'

I was startled to note that Nuggsy's mother, Amélie, was an extremely ravishing older woman. Lara had once told me that French women look up to a decade younger than their British counterparts, mainly due to early education around skincare maintenance. Mrs Nugget (Nugét) must have been in her fifties at least, in order to have a 35-year-old son, but her smooth, wrinkle-free visage ensured she didn't look a day over forty-five. She smiled at me and, ludicrous as it sounds, I felt an overwhelming urge to perform a curtsy. Before I knew it, I was down on one knee, introducing myself to Nuggsy's mother with a Victorian-era greeting.

'*Enchanté,*' I managed.

Amélie smiled demurely, allowing her hand to linger in mine before walking over to her son to provide a Parisian double-kiss on both cheeks.

'What the fuck are you doing, mate?' Nuggsy whispered incredulously as we walked over to the dinner table. 'You just fucking curtsied to my mum!'

'Mate, your fucking name is *Alain Nugét*?'

I swilled the glass of red wine, studying its form, admiring as the sediments fell gracefully toward the stem of the glass.

'What's this, Jean-Luc?' I enquired, testing out my own French pronunciation. I noticed Nuggsy give me a glare.

'Ah, this is a 2014 Cabernet Sauvignon from the Bordeaux Left Bank region. What do you think of it?'

I took another sip, savouring its complexity, the flavours dancing in my mouth.

'Mmm, it's just *divine*.'

Like the wine, conversation flowed freely, allowing me to learn more about the man behind the myth. Turned out Nuggsy's parents were currently living in Antibes (pronounced 'Ohn-teebe'), a beautiful resort town in the south of France between Nice and Cannes. They'd returned for a few months while Nuggsy's dad closed some kind of important business deal. The house we were dining in was an investment property-cum-holiday house, which they were planning to put back on the market in the next twelve months. I learned more about Jean-Luc and Amélie too, including how they'd met during the famous May 1968 protests, bonding over activism and a shared sense of adventure. Indeed, Nuggsy had inherited none of this political activism, unless you'd call his xenophobic *Fuck Off, We're Full* bumper sticker a form of political protest. That said, Nuggsy's first reaction to hearing the term 'Brexit' was 'did we play against that bloke in Greenies?', so I wasn't expecting an evening full of politically charged conversation.

Nuggsy's mother smiled at me. It was now abundantly clear she spoke very little English, if any.

'*Demande-lui comment vont ses études universitaires.*'

'Excuse me—err, *excusez-moi?*' I replied. '*Parlez-vous anglais?*'

'She asked how your university studies are going,' Nuggsy answered, not even looking up from his zucchini flower entrée.

Wait, Nuggsy speaks French?

'Well, things are going okay. I'm learning a bit about French existentialism at the moment, actually,' I answered, still rattled by the fact that Nuggsy was bilingual. Rattled by the fact his parents were French. Rattled by everything.

'Ahh, who are they focusing on? Sartre? De Beauvoir?' Mr Nugét asked.

'Actually, he's working at Outlaw Sport with Bretty. Remember Bretty, Dad?'

I'm not sure why Nuggsy felt compelled to belittle me in front of his parents, but I can only assume it was because the subject matter had dragged him out of his conversational comfort zone. To his credit, Jean-Luc looked to steer things in a fresh direction.

'Alain, can you please pass me the *champignons*?'

The conversation was spirited, lively, as we continued to jump effortlessly from musings on the recent French presidential election to the *Appellation d'Origine Contrôlée* status around French-produced cheeses. I could scarcely believe that these people had produced Alan Nugget. Or should I say, the preposterously named Alain Nugét.

Reclining into my seat, I sought to understand more about him.

'So, tell me about the young Alain as a boy. What was he *like*?' I asked, genuinely curious, like a girlfriend meeting her partner's family for the first time, keen to glean as much information as possible.

Jean-Luc reclined into his seat, a wistful smile creeping across his face.

'Well, we used to live in the countryside, just outside the town of Amiens, on an acreage not far from the famous World War I battlegrounds of the Somme. Alain grew up surrounded by beautiful meadows and rolling hills. We had several horses, and Alain—who was very small for his age—became an excellent rider.'

'Really?'

'Oh yes,' Mr Nugét continued, now in full nostalgia mode. 'Alain, what was the name of that horse you won the dressage competition with?'

Nuggsy's arms were crossed in a defiant display of body language.

'Can't remember, Papa.'

'Ah, I remember! It was Champagne!' Mr Nugét announced, beaming.

Between the *champignons* and his childhood horse, Champagne, I wondered whether this was where Nuggsy's long-held fascination with the word 'champ' had originated. Meanwhile, Amélie, who'd left the table for a moment, had returned with a bulky photo album under her arm. She flicked it open to a page that showcased six photos of the young Alain Nugét competing in a dressage tournament. He was wearing a little red jacket and white riding pants, a wild shock of blond hair peeking out from under a velvet hat. It was the first time I'd seen Nuggsy with hair. In these photos he appeared to have a soft European tan—much like his parents—which sat at odds with his current complexion. Years of playing grade cricket under the harsh Australian sun in ozone-depleted air had wreaked havoc on his skin.

'*Mon petit champion!*' Amélie purred affectionately.

'Mum, don't *champ* me!' Nuggsy hissed furiously, his expression a cocktail of wild hostility and pained embarrassment.

'So, what brought you guys to Australia?' I asked Jean-Luc.

'Well, I was offered a position at a prominent university. It seemed a good opportunity to bring the family over for a few years and experience a different culture. Alain was just eleven years old; we hoped he could improve his English, which would open up plenty of job opportunities when we returned home to France.'

As it turned out, Jean-Luc's work colleague had a son who played cricket, and Nuggsy was promptly signed up in his team.

'Alain was a natural sportsman and he learned the game very quickly. Before I knew it we were driving him all around the state every Saturday for various representative games.'

This was all fascinating information, which served to provide a fresh insight into the troubled mind of Nuggsy. On the surface, Nuggsy was the simplest person you've ever met: a tall bloke with a strong Australian accent and an insidious gambling addiction. This was the first time I'd ever lifted the veil on Alan Nugget's personal life. Much to my surprise, under the outgoing Aussie alpha-dog façade was a bilingual man with an EU passport. However, I couldn't help but notice a slight shift in energy in the room, as if I'd brought up something sensitive.

Jean-Luc continued on. 'A few years later, we were ready to return to France. I had finished up at the university, and Amélie and I were homesick. We missed good food and good wine. We wanted to return home to our friends and enrol Alain in a French private school, to secure his future. But at the time, Alain was playing, um, what was the under-16 competition called again, Alain?'

'*Greenies*, Dad. Green Shield,' Nuggsy answered, flatly. 'The most prestigious underage representative cricket competition in the state.'

'Ah, yes. This Green Shield competition. Alain was the leading wicket taker in the Green Shield that year. Someone—um, what was his name? I think it was Geoffrey. Yes, I remember now. Mr Beveridge. Anyway, Mr Beveridge called me one evening to say that Alain was a 'player of promise'—*un joueur prometteur*—and that he would one day play test cricket for Australia. He convinced Alain to sign up to his grade cricket club at the young age of sixteen ... and at that point, I knew we had lost him.'

Geoffrey Beveridge! Bevo! God, he'd been grooming Nuggsy for twenty years!

'We tried to get Alain to come with us. We told him to think of his future, that it was a huge risk to focus all his energy on playing cricket for Australia, but he wouldn't listen. In the end, he refused to come back with us to France, so we allowed him to stay out here. We returned to our homeland—and Alain hasn't been back to France since.'

I couldn't believe what I was hearing. Nuggsy had become so deeply ensconced in the world of grade cricket at such an impressionable young age—*sixteen!*—and, with the likes of Bevo in his ear telling him he was the 'future of Australian cricket', he'd turned his back on his French heritage in favour of Australian grade cricket. No wonder he clung to grade cricket like it was his life. For Nuggsy, grade cricket was family. It was his entire identity. I thought about my relationship with my own dad and how I'd been shaped by that experience. For years and years he'd driven me all around the state, paid my rego, given me throw downs after work, until a time came where he just couldn't do it any longer. All he really wanted was for me to succeed, only to watch me fail time and time again.

In an effort to change the subject once more, Nuggsy's mum tapped her wine glass three times and rose to her feet.

'*Un toast à mon fils, Alain, pour marquer cette occasion speciale.*'

Having recognised the words 'toast' and 'Alain', I took this to be Amélie's way of saluting Nuggsy's thirty-seventh birthday. We raised our glasses.

'*À ta santé!*'

But there was more to come as Jean-Luc took the floor.

'Alain,' he started, 'we've been giving this a lot of thought over the past couple of years ...' Mr Nugét cleared his throat as a faint quiver entered his voice. 'You know, we're not getting any younger. We want to make sure we can set you up for your future. We don't want to have to worry about you any longer.'

Nuggsy nodded sagely.

'As you know, my boy, I have had a rather successful career—I've been very lucky. Your grandfather was a very rich man and his inheritance has allowed us to make some very shrewd investments, which have reaped significant rewards over a long period of time.'

Nuggsy put down his fork, now offering Jean-Luc his full attention.

'Son, we've noticed some positive changes over the past couple of years. Even though we haven't been around to witness it firsthand, we can see that you're blossoming into a fine young man.'

Do they even know this bloke?

'Anyway, we believe that you are mature enough to manage your finances, which is why we will be making the first cash distribution to you as part of your trust fund. The balance will be paid out on your forty-fifth birthday.'

I looked over at Nuggsy, who hadn't said a word yet.

He didn't appear to have quite grasped all the words in the sentence.

'What are you saying, Papa?'

I couldn't believe it. Nuggsy was a trust fund baby. In truth, it went a long way towards explaining Nuggsy's mindset towards his finances. Presumably, he'd always known that one day the trust fund would be triggered. But now, having heard of his idyllic upbringing on the Somme, having seen the young Nuggsy resplendent in a silk dressage outfit—a vision of French old-money aristocracy—I felt duped, as if Nuggsy had sold me a lie all those years, even though he hadn't. A strange, sudden anger overwhelmed me.

Fuck this bloke!

'Nuggsy fixed grade cricket matches!' I blurted.

'*Comment?*' Amélie asked politely.

'Excuse me?' Mr Nugét shot back in an anxious tone, before turning to eyeball his son. 'Alain, what is this young man saying?'

Nuggsy looked at me with disbelief. Stunned, he sat there, mouth agape, completely lost for words. I genuinely hadn't meant to hang him out like that, even after he'd glee-fully revealed that I was working at a sports apparel store at the age of thirty-one. But obviously my latent anger over the match-fixing betrayal had never really subsided. We'd never properly addressed the 'incident' since living under the same roof. Yes, we'd drunk thousands of beers, been on dozens of circuits over the past month or so, but never had we had a serious conversation about what went down that day—or about anything, really. I'd tried to engage in multiple deep and meaningful talks with Nuggsy over the years—career progression, relationships, global warming—but never really got anywhere. To be fair, once we spent four hours discussing my crippling fear of the short ball. He did offer some helpful advice that evening, but the very next training session he was actively bumping me off seventeen yards in the nets with a two-piecer that he'd managed to procure from somewhere. 'This bloke *hates* the short ball!' he yelped, before encouraging our first grade quick to share his new pill and attack my rib cage in fast-fading light on a deck that was half-mud half-pitch.

Nuggsy's dad switched back to his native tongue, where he appeared much more at home.

'*Explique-toi! Immédiatement!*'

'Papa, *je peux tout expliquer!*'

'Um, guys,' I interrupted, 'do you mind speaking in English?'

I was keen to be across all this myself. Nuggsy composed himself and continued.

'Okay, Papa. Look, it's true. A few years ago I was involved in a match-fixing ring. I was low on cash and it seemed like a good way to pay off some debts. You guys were living over in Antibes'—he pronounced it perfectly as 'Ohn-teebe'—'and I didn't have anyone to fall back on, so I did the only thing I *could* do: conspire with a man in his sixties to arrange predetermined outcomes in lower grade cricket matches.'

'What? You were *what*? Who was this man?' Jean-Luc fumed.

'I know, I know, it sounds highly unlikely. Almost as if this entire storyline is a ridiculous work of fiction. Me and

Geoffrey—you know, Mr Beveridge—well, we plotted together to fix grade cricket matches. I pocketed around $46,000 over the course of three seasons, but it's all gone now.'

As I'd suspected, Nuggsy's match-fixing wasn't a one-off event. It was a highly sophisticated covert operation that had taken place across several years, indirectly involving hundreds of unsuspecting cricketers. Bevo had groomed Nuggsy from the get-go. How many averages had been inflated, bowling figures destroyed, grade cricket careers ruined as a result of this nefarious scheme? What's more, I had played alongside Nuggsy in every single match across that three-year period. I felt the hatred rising up inside me once more, but forced myself to stay silent. This was a pivotal moment between a son and his parents—a brutal confession, a baring of the soul—and I had to let it play out.

Mr Nugét turned to his wife and explained, in whispered French, the details of Nuggsy's sin. She gasped in horror, drawing a delicate hand to her mouth before shaking her head slowly.

'*Je suis tellement déçue,*' she uttered, voice trembling.

I didn't need Google Translate to tell me that Mrs Nugét was severely disappointed in her only son.

Mr Nugét put a consoling arm around his wife, while Nuggsy leaned over to me and whispered.

'Mate, why on earth would you bring that up?'

I had nothing to say. Nuggsy pressed, tears welling.

'Just . . . why?'

I was about to try to respond—with what, I'm not sure— when Jean-Luc cleared his throat, his arm still around a now sobbing Amélie.

'I'm sorry to cut the night short, but I think we need to discuss this revelation further as a family. Can I call you a taxi?'

I rose from the table and surveyed the carnage. Nuggsy was sitting head bowed, gently rocking back and forth on his seat. Jean-Luc and Amélie were huddled together on the other side of the table. My candour had triggered a family crisis.

What have I done?

'No, it's okay, I'll see myself out. Thanks so much for a wonderful evening. Umm, see you at home, Nuggsy?'

Nuggsy, still looking down, replied in a barely audible whisper.

'Yeah, mate. See you at home.'

13

BROKEN

Out of nowhere, a phone call changed everything. Most people see that as reason to avoid answering, but I've always taken a different view. It's not that I'm addicted to my phone, I just think it may be giving me an opportunity. Somebody wants to talk to me. They need me for something. I am required. It never fails to elicit a minor thrill when I get a call from a private or unknown number, and this day was no different. How I would come to rue it.

On the other end was a man named Arthur Bowen, chief administrator of the recently renamed Premier Cricket competition. He introduced himself as such. He needn't have—I knew who he was. Arthur was known as the bureaucrats' bureaucrat of grade (premier) cricket, a classic administrator whose mitts could be found on every new regulation and rule change in the game. He loved cosying up to first graders and other administrative suits. It was never clear whether the sycophancy was returned. Years ago, he was clearly bald; now he had hair—courtesy of a transplant, or plugs, as overt as a sexual advance from Donald Trump in the nineties. He sounded every bit as grave and officious as the reputation that preceded him.

'Hello. I am calling in relation to an incident eighteen months ago in the third grade grand final.'

I froze. The voice continued.

'I wish to inform you that you have been summoned to Premier Cricket's peak judiciary body to answer a charge of match-fixing for financial benefit. Before you respond, I want to let you know that this is a matter of the utmost seriousness. Should you be found guilty, you may face a lifetime ban from cricket, and a significant fine for bringing the game into disrepute.'

I remained silent. I knew exactly what he was referring to, but I couldn't allow it to seem that way.

'Do you have anything to say?' Arthur asked.

'I . . . I'm shocked. I don't know what this is about,' I eventually stammered, heart pounding.

'I'm sure you are, son,' he continued. 'You are required to attend the judiciary hearing tomorrow at 6.30 p.m. sharp. I suggest you familiarise yourself with judiciary protocol ahead of your appearance. I must warn you that the prosecution would not be bringing this case without a sufficient body of evidence. I suggest you carefully consider your plea.'

And with that, he was gone. Everything was a blur afterward, and before I knew it I was suited and ready for court. As I combed my ever-thinning hair, I couldn't help but think

I looked pretty good in my suit too. *Don't look half bad in a bag of fruit*, I thought, out of habit more than anything. I admonished myself immediately.

Premier Cricket's judiciary room was far more imposing than I'd imagined. Old mahogany pillars surrounded the dock and a highly perched chair for the sitting judge, Richard Silverman QC. There was even a witness box, with two tables set up in the same formation as an actual court. It all appeared a bit much for something as relatively insignificant as grade cricket. But again, perhaps this was all part of elevating the status of Premier Cricket.

'All rise,' barked some weedy bloke, performing a nondescript administrative role to start things.

Arthur Bowen sat at a panel-style table, his plugged hair swept over in a manner that would do Narcissus proud. As it transpired, he was the prosecution too, a fact he had failed to mention over the phone. Wasn't that grounds for objection, or some shit? Whatever the case, he was openly revelling in the officialdom of it all. To my left was my representation, Jean-Luc Nugét, aka Nuggsy's dad. I hadn't expected anyone to help me, but he had turned up unannounced. I was forever indebted to him, though it begged the question: if I was here, and Nuggsy's dad was here, then where on earth was Nuggsy? I thought I'd seen him flash by outside of court, but he wasn't in the room. Perhaps he'd been missed in the whole investigation. Or had he dobbed me in as part of some plea bargain, or some evil redemption for putting his trust fund activation at risk of delay? Maybe he really *had* given me up, and sent his dad to help out as a guilty consolation. I tried not to get ahead of myself.

I turned around to the viewing area. Why on earth *was* there a viewing area, complete with gallery, in a Premier Cricket judiciary room? And why were so many people here to see this? As I scanned the room, I caught some familiar faces. Old teammates: Bretty, Bruiser, Nathan, just to name a few. How did they even know about this? Even though they'd presumably come along in support, each of their heads was bowed as they strived to avoid eye contact. At this, my heart sank, and it was now that the waves of shame began. That familiar lump in my throat rose sharply as I looked around the room.

That's when I saw Dad.

Unlike the others, he had no problem with eye contact. I expected an expression somewhere on the spectrum of anger and disappointment, but it was worse than that. His eyes told of an unspeakable sadness, etched onto his face as evocatively as in an original Banksy. Though, unlike the work of the mysterious artist, this time I knew how it got there. The magnitude of my match-fixing collusion with Nuggsy had weighed profoundly on my conscience for so long, and now I would receive my comeuppance. Everybody in the room, as far as I could tell, had already judged me. I instantly thought of Lara, the one person who I knew would have stood by me if she were here. *She* would know the truth of it—that I only did it to help Nuggsy, that I'd changed my mind midway through the fix, that I had some character to show for it. But, sadly, she wasn't here.

'Will the defendant please rise?' Judge Silverman bellowed to commence proceedings.

Nervously, I rose to my feet.

'You are here on charges of match-fixing for financial benefit. The charge relates to your involvement in the third grade grand final of two seasons prior. We are here to establish whether you in fact fixed the result in question and, if so, whether you gained financially from it. This is unprecedented in cricket at this level. It is a grave charge, indeed.'

I gulped at his use of the phrase 'grave charge'.

'So, how do you plea?'

'H-how do I plea?'

Mr Nugét gave me a nudge, as if to suggest I should comply.

'Sorry, Your . . . Honour. Not guilty. I am not guilty of match-fixing. I didn't fix that match,' I finally finished.

'So be it,' Silverman said curtly.

He turned to face Arthur Bowen and gave him a nod. Bowen responded with a smug, knowing nod of his own. Silverman continued.

'Arthur, as prosecution, please make your opening remarks.'

'No problem, Richard. With pleasure.'

Richard Silverman QC smiled. Why was Arthur allowed to call him Richard? This seemed a fix of its own.

'Ladies and gentlemen of the Premier Cricket community, I thank you for coming this evening. In coming here you have established a record attendance for a judiciary hearing, and it is understandable. Tonight, I will demonstrate to you how the actions of one man constitute an attack on the fabric of the game itself. Sadly, we are all too aware of the perils of match-fixing in the professional realm of the game. But never, ever did we consider that this plague would infest the club scene. Especially *third grade!*'

The comment about third grade drew wry chuckles from the courtroom. I mean, I was humiliated enough as it was, but this? With the onlookers on his side now, Arthur pressed on.

'Almost two years ago, the man who sits before you agreed to perform in such a manner as to ensure his team lost the grand final. With the match almost won, he conceded 41 runs from 11 deliveries to consign his team to defeat. For his efforts, he pocketed ten thousand dollars.'

Arthur was strolling the court now.

'OBJECTION!' I yelled out. 'What about my 66 off 31 balls? How do you explain that, champ? Fuck me, there wouldn't have been the chance of a win without it! Seriously, what's *doing* here?'

Now I was out of my own chair.

'Quiet!' said Mr Nugét. 'Your time will come.'

He motioned to the judge that I would not interrupt any further.

'Yes, it certainly *was* interesting that you had a strike rate of 213 that day, wasn't it?' Arthur continued, looking at me. 'In fact, I have your MyCricket statistics in front of me. Your previous best strike rate for an innings above 10—and there aren't too many, I might add—was 45. For a man with forearms as weak as yours—a middling rig, at best—this seems highly suspicious. Is it possible you were *trying* to get out, but got lucky?'

He let the question linger for a long time. I presumed the question was rhetorical.

'Well, was it? Cat got your tongue?' he said.

The crowd of onlookers snickered. This wasn't going well.

'I-I-I just thought you were asking a rhetor—'

'Or,' he said, cutting me off to regain control of the argument, 'does your associate *Bevo* have your tongue?'

I was stunned by both the mention of Bevo and the strange metaphor of him having my tongue. Clearly, Arthur knew something.

'You see, ladies and gentlemen,' he went on, walking the aisle that separated the audience and speaking to them with the charisma of Hortensius, the great orator of Ancient Rome, 'our friend here had closely guarded business dealings with the man his associates called "Bevo", or Geoffrey Beveridge, as he is formally known.'

This was bad news.

'At this point in time our friend here may be thinking, *I might just have beaten this*. After all, Geoffrey is sadly no longer with us. But before Geoffrey succumbed to cirrhosis of the liver, he confessed everything to me. On his deathbed, no less. The meeting at McDonald's, the agreement to throw the game, the exchange of funds into your Commonwealth Dollarmite account . . .'

Arthur continued. 'He had a heavy conscience, did Geoffrey, and he alleviated it of guilt right before he died.'

An audible gasp emanated from the gallery.

'Do you have anything to say now?' Arthur challenged.

I scanned the room again, heart ready to burst through my chest, hands clammy and sweaty, tie loosened. Everybody was staring at me now, nodding their heads in perfect rhythm. This was it. This was how cricket was going to finish for me. In disgrace, acrimony. Dad's face was even sadder than before, and then I saw my mum. She never came to cricket, but she knew *this* was wrong. She was in tears, inconsolable. And, wait, was that ... was that *Lara*? Smiling at me?

I shot up from bed, drenched in sweat, breathing short, shallow breaths. The room was dark, my brain hazy. The courtroom ... Arthur Bowen as Hortensius ... heads bowed ... Jean-Luc Nugét ... Lara ... Nuggsy conspicuously absent ...

I was not going to grade cricket jail. I was going to be okay.

I would be up in three hours to play the last game of the season. Even in my dreams, cricket was still fucking with me.

At the end of a gruelling year, there was still the final game to negotiate. I'd slept poorly; the previous night's bad dream had stirred something in me. What, exactly, I wasn't sure. I was guilty and I had a heavy heart—maybe this intensity would help me in the final game of the year? Perhaps I could leverage this emotional anguish for a gritty 30-odd? Fuck, I was tired, though. Emotionally and physically exhausted.

I'd be making my own way to the ground this morning, since earlier in the week Nuggsy had declared himself unavailable for the final game of the season. A few days later he'd flown out to visit his parents in France. It was an open-ended ticket, which made me wonder whether this was the last I'd seen of my good friend Alain Nugét. It was a shock to all, considering his record of never missing a single cricket match in ten years, although not to me. Around the house, the frost had not thawed since that fateful dinner with Nuggsy's parents. We'd barely spoken in the weeks after, tiptoeing around each other in the kitchen and largely avoiding each other at training. Our once great friendship now in turmoil.

Once thing was for sure, though: Saturday mornings just weren't the same without him around. Today was 35 degrees, the sort of day that really brought out the wafts of dried sweat and worn upholstery in Nuggsy's 24-year-old car. On days like this I'd feel the rush of heat upon lowering myself into the car, moving four sticky bottles of Gatorade aside to do so. But Nuggsy wasn't here driving me to the game; he was in the beautiful town of Amiens, reconnecting with his French heritage in the countryside. I didn't have a car of my own so I was forced to take three forms of public transport in order to get to the game. At least it gave me plenty of time to contemplate the match ahead.

Come on, mate, runs today.

Of course, I was late. Three minutes late. Not one minute late, which allows you to argue yourself out of a fine, based on slight variability in watches, but three. Close enough that you reflect on small details, far enough that you're down sixty sheets because of the case you're now obligated to buy. The echoes of Fazza—the handsome private school kid who'd been moved to my position at six thus relegating me to seven—yelling 'Result!' just made it worse. Deep house music was blasting out of Fazza's portable speaker; ten years ago you could bank on pre-match music that contained some skerrick of a melody. Now I had to contend with buying a case that this fuckwit would profit from, probably to the soundtrack of trance in a suburban dressing-room. It was enough to make me physically shudder.

Still, runs would fix everything. Runs always fix everything.

We ventured out for the standard pre-match warm-up to find the other side already out there, immersing themselves in some engaging hybrid warm-up game that served the multilayered purpose of building camaraderie, loosening their limbs and, most importantly, intimidating the opposition. They say cricket is won and lost between the ears. Obviously, that's bullshit—it's won before the game even commences. The main reason for being on the field at all in the hour before play is to critically analyse the opposition. It's all done out of the corner of the eye, naturally, but it's done in earnest.

Our team wasn't imaginative enough to invent a warm-up game of its own so we started off with fielding drills. The most generic fielding drill in cricket is the one where someone (usually the captain) hits you one along the ground. Just as you pick the ball up to return it to the keeper, he hits another ball to you in the air. The aim, I think, is to hone your spatial awareness, but it's without doubt one of the most stupid, pseudo-clever fielding drills that exists. The net result is that the player will rush the throw (for fear of being hit on the head by a ball-missile) and struggle to get into a good position to effect the catch. Since only one player can be involved in the drill at any one time, there are usually eight or ten other blokes milling behind doing absolutely nothing. As fielding drills go, it's a masterclass in inefficiency.

We followed the fielding drills with a series of throw downs, which were ultimately made redundant the moment Snooker lost the toss, ensuring we would bowl first. In these situations, there's always some precious bloke who still insists on hitting up. Today it was Crooksy, who requested that I throw him a couple while the rest of the team continued their fielding drills. Crooksy was a heavy-set left-hander averaging 12.6 this season, but he'd played a few games in first grade several years back, which had led him to believe he was entitled to throw downs on demand. I reluctantly agreed to Crooksy's request on the basis that I'd get a set of throw downs in return, but I was nervous. I have reason to be scared of being whacked by a batsman during throw downs because, well, that's precisely what *I* do when I'm batting. Any batsman worth their salt who denies trying to hit the 'giver' every so often is a liar, and in my view, not a real batsman.

As expected, Crooksy smoked a straight one directly at my shins; the ball sped off his blade towards me like a tracer bullet. Like a skater wearing Vans grinding a handrail in 1997, I tried to jump out of the way but failed. The ball smashed into my right shin and ricocheted straight back to Crooksy, who, without irony, executed a copybook off drive in the direction of the opposition. As the thrower, it was my duty to go and fetch the ball. I limped over to ask for it, but they all shrugged their shoulders and claimed not to have seen it. Again, I've been that person before, and all you're doing is stealing a cricket ball.

Runs fix everything. Runs always fix everything.

I trudged into the rooms trying to stay positive. More deep house music blasted on a stereo system that belonged to one of the young blokes, whose name I was yet to learn. Adding to the noise was Snooker, barking instructions on how to get the ball to 'reverse'. Part of me wanted to interrupt him to clarify that none of us knew how to get the ball reversing, nor would we have the know-how to capitalise if it did, by some miracle, start to 'go'. Cricketers who claim to understand the science behind swing bowling are inevitably the least likely to execute such principles. An old teammate of mine, John, wrote forty thousand words on 'Bernoulli's Principle of Fluid Dynamics' for his physics thesis, yet the bloke still couldn't bowl a fucking outswinger. I blocked this all out and turned my attention to finding some sunscreen. I didn't have any of my own (why would I—I've only played cricket my entire life) so I walked over to the new bloke, Chris, who was busily creaming up in the corner.

'Mate, mind if I use a bit of that?'

'Umm . . . do you have three dollars?'

'Wait, what?'

Chris shifted uneasily as he measured his response.

'Look, mate, this stuff is expensive. It's fifty-plus sunscreen. Sets me back about twenty-five dollars. If half the team use it every week, I'm basically paying twenty-five dollars a match to wear sunscreen. Now, that's a little silly, isn't it?'

Both his maths and his reasoning were spot-on, but I'd never heard of a player *charging* someone for sunscreen. With the umpire already on his way out, time was of the essence, so I reluctantly paid Chris with the five-dollar note I had. He promptly returned four fifty-cent pieces to me, which somehow seemed more degrading than had he given no change. As I ran the translucent sunscreen over my face and forearms, it became immediately obvious that this cheap, runny shit was not fifty-plus protection. Alpha'd, once again.

The sunscreen thing wasn't the end of it, though. Upon opening my kit to get changed, it dawned on me: I'd forgotten my whites. The one thing I needed to bring in order to participate in the fixture. I foraged frantically through my bag, hoping by some divine intervention they'd show up. Alas, there I stood, shirtless in my training shorts, heart pounding, caught in one of cricket's most embarrassing situations. The rest of the team was changed and ready. I decided that my play was to act lighthearted about it, even though I was ready to break down in tears.

'Lads. Don't, ahhh ... suppose anyone, ahhh ... has a spare pair of whites, do they?'

The room fell silent. I looked around at my teammates—most of them couldn't have been over twenty years old. Since they were so young, the majority of them still lived at home with their parents, which meant they were all wearing crisp, clean whites, lovingly washed by their respective mothers. Again, another example of the shifting demographics of grade cricket. Back in the day, my teammates were a bit older, lived together in share houses that resembled crack dens, and wore dirty, grass-stained creams that had been marinating in their kits all week. It was a simpler time. Now, all I saw were vacant nods and a liberal smattering of smirks.

'Mate,' Stodge started, 'you're going to have to ask the opposition, I think.'

I could sense the room tense up at the prospect of that humiliation.

'No way, Stodge. No fucking way.'

His suggestion was horrifying, but to be fair, there weren't many alternatives. It was too late for me to dash home and grab them. For starters, I didn't have a car. All of a sudden, a vision of Nuggsy and Bruiser, laughing maniacally, popped into my head. Specifically, their reaction to Emma's walk of shame, where she'd strolled out of the house in full whites on her way to cricket. Actually, where the fuck *were* my whites, anyway? I hadn't washed them, so they should logically still have been in my kit. Had Nuggsy taken them out before he left, one final act of sabotage? Had Emma stolen them too, along with my hat-trick trophy? Fuck, yet another fear-based dream to add to the list. Fear of getting timed out. Fear of being outed as an accessory to match-fixing. Fear of losing my whites. Fuckloads of fear, all of it emotionally deep-seated.

'Nah, you better head there and ask, mate,' Stodge continued, digging in his heels. 'We've got to go. Umpire's already on his way.'

God, I had no choice, did I? I walked over to the opposition door and peeked inside. The players were sitting around chatting boisterously, in various stages of undress, save for the padded-up top order batsmen. The atmosphere was confident, relaxed. I knocked on the door and stepped through tentatively. Immediately, the room fell silent, as if I was an out-of-towner stepping into a saloon in the Old West.

'Lads, um, sorry about this but don't suppose someone has a pair of whites I might be able to borrow?'

I could make out a suppressed 'oh my God' from one of the players. But aside from that, no one else said a word as I stood there, shirtless, shoeless, in nothing more than training shorts, pleading with my opponents for a spare set of whites. A good thirty seconds passed before their opening batsmen finally rose and walked out the door to go and bat. The message was clear: no, mate, we don't have a spare set of whites.

It had been a fucking grim start to the day, even by usual standards. I'd copped a fine on arrival and been goaded by a handsome private school student ten years my junior. I'd been smacked on the shin by a teammate who failed to apologise for causing my pain. I'd paid three dollars for sunscreen just so I could try to avoid getting sunburnt on a 35-degree day. And I'd forgotten my cricket whites. Nobody, at any stage, had assisted me. Seriously, what the fuck was I even doing here? I always used to joke about how cricket deprived me of my Saturdays. How I'd never been to a farmer's market. How I hadn't been to the beach since 1997. I was comfortable missing out on all these normal weekend activities, though, because I was playing the sport I loved, surrounded by familiar faces. We were all failing, together. Again, those faces—Nuggsy, Damo, Bruiser, Deeks, Timbo, Swampy, Bretty, Robbo, Wazza—ran through my head. Bretty's stories. Damo's cover drive. Bruiser's money. Robbo's crippling addiction to Taiwanese prostitutes. Of that old brigade, I never once thought I'd be the last man standing, but here I was, still playing grade cricket, still wasting my weekends.

Back in the room, the scene was essentially the same as before, and everyone wanted to know the verdict. Had I been successful in procuring a pair of whites from the enemy? I looked around at my teammates, a bouquet of young, fresh faces, each with perfect zinc application; each with matching apparel and Fitness First rig to boot. The deep house music continued to throb endlessly in the background. The umpire was already out on the field. It was time to go. Everyone was awaiting my move. So, I made one. I calmly placed my training shirt in my kit, zipped it up, then wheeled it out of the sheds and began my slow walk to the nearby train station in full view of the opposition. I heard the cheers as I looped all the way around the field to stop at a pedestrian crossing, but I wasn't looking back, not for a second. The green light flashed, and I crossed the busy road, still shirtless. Where was I going? Who knew. Who cared?

All I knew was that I was never, ever coming back to cricket. This time, I was truly done.

14

A DIFFERENT WAY

I paced through the labyrinth of passageways to get to the platform, jostling my way through similarly faceless, rain-sodden people. Upon arrival, I had a rare moment to stop and wipe the excess raindrops from my overcoat. The train would be here soon. You always see its lights before it arrives. It was 6 p.m., or thereabouts, and as the glimmer curved around the tunnel, eventually giving way to the actual train, I readied myself to file in to the carriage with the head-down shuffle rhythm I'd become accustomed to. Here, with so many people around, no other style of stride was possible. It was a shuffle emblematic of our collective energy, sapped after yet another nine-to-five, with barely the vigour to do much more than drag ourselves on. Minding the gap, of course. We were weary commuters all, ready to endure another sardined experience en route to home.

A few months ago, this scene would have provoked an unshakeable restlessness in me. The crowds of people, the lack of space, the mini-alpha moments that public transport throws up so well. Beneath a neutral gaze, my mind would have run silently rampant.

Oh, you need to push in front of me, do you? To get onto a train that we're both going to board in a second? Yep, you go first. Shoulder me, bump me, jostle me. You want it more. You get what you want. Go on, take the space. Make it yours. Make me readjust to something else. It's dog eat dog here, isn't it? Not just train positioning. Life. Your agenda is more important than mine. You're prepared to leverage me to win. Your attitude is why people regard you as successful. It's why they regard me as a pushover. Well done. I'll just press my face against the window for balance.

Or:

Yeah, that's right, stand two abreast down the escalator to the platform. Even though people are rushing home, it's more important that you observe each other from equal height than allow people to move at their own pace. We will wait while you two talk about something else. It'll be inane, no doubt. You will see us all impatiently waiting in your periphery. It will make no difference, because you need to have your conversation.

Or:

Even though we're both squashed on the train, you'd like me to start moving for you now, lest you mightn't exit in time? You want me to find other handrails while the train travels at 150 kilometres per hour, because of your unfounded anxiety that you won't find a route off? Have you ever seen anyone miss their stop because it's too crowded to get off? No? You haven't? No worries, I'll risk falling and bumping others so that you can manage your irrational angst. I might offer a meagre hip-and-shoulder as you pass—you'll barely feel it, but I'll inflate the nature of the contact to my mates when I next speak to them.

On and on it would go. But now, jammed up against a microcosm of the entire CBD, I didn't mind. Those thoughts were there—they would always be there—but I found them gently amusing more than anything else.

'The next station is Euston,' soothed the automated female voiceover. 'Change here for the Northern line. And National Rail Service.'

I was in London. I'd moved here a few months ago, somewhat hastily, because I needed to get away. It was a vague reason then, and it still feels vague now. Whatever it was, I knew I needed a comprehensive change from home. I could work out the reasons later. I'd managed to find some work in London before I came over. In the course of my time at Outlaw Sport, I'd come across various sales representatives looking to flog product. It was rare for them to come into the retail store itself, but sometimes they had to drop their gear off. One of those guys was Harry Sharpton; he represented a British bat manufacturer called Woodcraft and Co. Sharpton was an executive director of this prestigious UK company and had come to Australia personally to understand the market ahead of a push into what he mysteriously called 'APAC'. He wanted to see how the product moved 'end to end', and that's how we came across each other on the floors of Outlaw—the end of all ends, I imagined.

'These are good sticks,' I'd said to him at the store. 'Decent pick-up, good weighting.'

I'd had no idea what I was talking about, really, and I didn't know what 'good weighting' actually meant, but I did like the stickers on the bat, and the wood had nice mesmerising lines on it, so I deduced that it was probably a good blade. After he requested I stop 'pulverising the toe into the ground' (in my defence, I was only facing up in a short innings of shadow batting while he was talking to me), we had a better conversation about the marriage of sport and business. He was well dressed, well spoken, and clearly had the resources to travel to Australia to flog sticks, so I asked him outright whether he made good coin doing it, and how he'd managed to make it global.

'Well,' he started, 'first, you need to understand what business you're in. You may think I'm in the cricket business. I'm not.'

He'd let the sentence hang, watching me at all times with a furrowed brow.

'Well, what industry are you in?' I queried, genuinely engaging with this suave Englishman who owned factories of bespoke sticks but wasn't selling cricket.

'I'm in the toy industry, my good man. These things are toys. Once you understand that, you understand how much potential this business has.

'I don't know a thing about cricket. I don't need to. I just know how to shape good-quality wood and make things look nice. We change the shapes of bats every year. It's just like fashion. Trends come in and out. Last year, lower middles were in. This year, it's a little higher.'

I was amazed.

'Is that why I hear players saying they prefer bats that

are two-pounds-ten now, whereas three years ago people liked two-pounds-nine?' I asked earnestly.

'That's a perfect example,' he'd replied, before handing me his business card. 'We're looking to expand into APAC in the next two-to-three years. You have a good sense of curiosity about you—and that's all I need. If you're ever interested in learning more, get in touch. Perhaps there will be an opportunity to build the business here later.'

Three months later, I'd secured my Tier 2 (General) visa to the UK. I would defer university, and learn the bat/toy-making business with Harry, before returning to build the business at home. Truth be known, I wasn't at all interested in staying close to cricket. Harry's assertion that this was really about toys and fashion had blown my mind, and I dreamed of becoming a well-dressed mogul, just like him. The fact I knew something about cricket helped, but I was pushing that as far away from my consciousness as possible. So, in a bout of courage, I upped and left for a city seventeen thousand kilometres from home, family and friends, on the other side of the world. That's how I described it on Facebook, anyway, to 121 likes and 13 comments.

While London is a great distance from Australia, it's almost like moving to another Australian city. You can think yourself as intrepid as you want, but when you move to London in your thirties you're likely to have more Australian friends there than you did back home. And then, when you go out after a week at work, you will probably hang out with other intrepid people—all Australian, of course. You will talk to each other about how good London is, how cosmopolitan, all while remaining in your enclave of

Australians, tut-tutting about the sheer backwardness of matters at home.

Anyway, I was living in Brixton, a place with great character though experiencing rapid gentrification at the expense of true locals. Even though I was an outsider on a good wage, I never once considered that I was part of that gentrification. I would merely sit in the confines of the hipster-central Pop Brixton and pontificate on the tragedy of *other* outsiders killing the local culture while drinking internationally sourced boutique coffee or craft beer. London had a greater buzz than any city in Australia, but I felt at peace here. I took solace in my anonymity, and was particularly glad to be away from the incestuous grade cricket scene. Don't get me wrong, I still received multiple texts and inbox messages plainly asking 'How's the circuit?', so I hadn't full extricated myself from the steel jaws of the cricketing fraternity, but I was far enough away that I didn't have to 'champ' my way through every social interaction with males who play sport on a daily basis. That was a relief.

I thought about all of this as I rode my way home on the Victoria line—a magnificent journey if you can ignore the crowds—and wondered what I'd be doing if I was home in Australia. It was 6 p.m. on a Thursday. I'd probably be making my way to training, internally strategising about how I might jag an early net. I'd be wondering if there'd be any decent cricket balls remaining in the club stash, and how many I'd pilfered over the years. I'd be wondering whether we had fitness that night, and whether I had sufficient age or social capital to give it a miss. I'd be thinking about our last club coach, who used to take sick pleasure in making

fitness as mundane as possible. He would have us continu-
ally sprint around the infield 'ring', with thirty-second rests
in between. No cricket balls, no competition, no stakes, no
fun. Just young adults running around in circles until they
vomited. When we'd rest, he'd deny us water. 'Water's weak,'
he'd say. 'We're too weak at this club,' he'd go on. 'Look
at you all. You bat for twenty minutes and want a second
pair of gloves and a drink. You don't work hard enough.
You're too soft. Water? You have to earn it.' That broke me
a little. When drinking water was considered weak, I knew
I'd never attain the hardness I always craved.

But instead of thinking about those things, I was now
reading Charles Dickens' *Great Expectations* on my Kindle.
Frankly, I was astonished that a book written in 1860 could
so elegantly reflect class attitudes in England today. I'd only
previously thought of social hierarchy through the prism
of first graders, lower graders, Shires cricketers and park
cricketers. *Great Expectations'* hero, Pip Pirrip, was effectively a park cricketer, and his story opened my mind to the
truth that park cricketers are indeed real people too.

I eagerly checked my phone upon exiting Brixton
station. Even though I had my book, no mobile network in
the underground had meant thirty painful minutes without
internet, and I'd been suffering what doctors would no
doubt call genuine withdrawal symptoms. I wasn't worried
about my internet addiction, though. To my surprise, I had
an actual message. It was from an unknown number—
the best kind of text. It read: *Hey, heard you were in London.
I've been here a little while too. Would love to get a coffee with
you. No agendas. Would just be nice to say hello. Lara.*

A few months ago, that text would have floored me. I would have analysed each sentence, filled myself with paranoia about every choice of word. I would have drafted and redrafted my reply. But not now. I looked at it, took it at face value, smiled, and wrote back quickly.

Hey Lara, nice to hear from you! Coffee sounds great. I'm in Brixton, happy to go anywhere. Where/when?

Her reply was quick.

I know a nice spot in Beckenham. It's a little south of London but not too far. BR31AY. How's this Saturday afternoon? Unless you have cricket?

I was equally quick to reply.

Sounds great, I'll be there. I hate cricket. Never playing again. See you Sat.

Her nonchalant use of the UK postcode system suggested she'd been here a while, while the cricket question was probably fair. I moseyed to my share house feeling relaxed, already looking forward to Saturday with the purity of someone who didn't feel any great pull towards their ex-girlfriend but, rather, a genuine enthusiasm for seeing someone I knew well. Once home, I thought no more of it. I got ready for trivia and had a great time drinking pints and feeling intellectually inferior to English people, which—as an Australian—was just how they liked me, I suspected.

I made my way to Beckenham via the overground train and took a quick jaunt up High Street to a cafe called Fee &

Brown. It had a minimalist cool to it: was boutique enough to satisfy my smug Australian cafe sensibilities but understated enough to avoid feeling like an overblown hipster commune. Lara always did have good taste.

Lara was also always notoriously late, and today was no exception. I saw her before she saw me, breezing past the window with earphones in, radiant as ever. She opened the door for an old gent who was exiting, and I stood and said hello once she'd come in. We hugged, smiled, and everything felt friendly. There were no pangs of pain or heartbreak, just acceptance that life had had its way with us. Don't get me wrong, I was as nervous as anything, but I felt mature somehow.

To continue my newfound maturity, I told Lara that she looked lovely, which she did.

'You're looking really well—it's great to see you,' I said.

'Oh, thank you! That's very nice of you to say!' she replied, both surprised and flattered by my sincerity.

'Is that dress and jacket Marimekko?'

'Wow,' she said. 'When did you develop such attention to detail? As a matter of fact, they are!'

Emboldened, I kept going. 'I know we're going to catch up etcetera, but can I just ask: when you pick clothes, do you try to match brands? Or, even better, coordinate your clothing so you're just wearing *all* of the same brand? I guess it's kind of like those players who want to look sponsored in cricket—you match everything so your kit looks synthesised. It gives you this indescribable feeling of symmetry, which is the key to beauty, you know? Anyway, do you try to look sponsored when you dress?'

Lara looked at me for a second, deeply. I sensed that something was a bit amiss—that I'd done something strange. Then she burst out laughing.

'Oh my God!' she said, almost wiping tears away, so much was she in fits of laughter. 'You told me you *hated* cricket the other day. But you still love it, don't you?'

I think my comment had released the tension in some way. After so much time away from each other, with so much change in our lives, here I was, understanding her fashion sense through lazy cricket analogies. She seemed amused by it, thankfully, and not perturbed at all.

'I'm sorry. I guess I'm a bit nervous. You know how I get,' I offered sheepishly.

'Don't worry,' she replied, her laughter finally subsiding. 'I know you have these reflexes when you're nervous. You're just trying to connect—even if you have inadvertently compared me to an insecure grade cricketer.'

'Thanks for understanding,' I mustered.

And so kicked off an hour of absorbing 'catch up'. Lara finished her volunteering program and had come over to commence a doctorate in clinical psychology at King's College. She told me about her time in Guatemala, where she quickly found that the program she'd signed up to had no authority with local Guatemalan people.

'I think the course coordinators presumed they'd be wanted because they were white and rich,' she said. 'And even when the program wasn't working too well, the leaders kept asking me about my relationship with God, and whether or not I'd join their Bible study after work.'

Those volunteers who joined Bible study would tend to

be given the most interesting work during the day. Kind of like when the captain is desperate for you to have a beer with him after training. You don't want it, least of all with him, but you're teetering on the brink of being dropped so you head along. But despite the program's Christian edge, Lara found the experience worthwhile, and completed the full six months before flying to London and moving into her own share house with some girls in Clapham Junction, where she'd been for a few months. There was no talk of another bloke, and I didn't want to bring it up. I was more than happy to remain in the dark about it.

During that time we'd worked our way through some second-rate smashed avocado and non-artisan coffee, barely pausing as Lara talked about the unintended arrogance of some foreign programs from Western nations, arriving to save locals who haven't asked for their help. The conversation was so engrossing that we'd barely noticed the place had already started to pack up. The reticent cafe staff had begun packing chairs onto the vacant tables, which was our cue to leave.

'I've barely had a chance to ask about you. I know a nice walk around here. Got time?' Lara said.

'Yeah, sounds good,' I replied.

Once we'd paid, we commenced our leisurely amble down the cobbled High Street path.

'So,' Lara began. 'What's the deal with cricket? You're here? You're not playing at home? What happened to that?'

I was conscious of wanting to avoid launching into a flurry of angst about what had happened—more out of shame than anything else. Lara had a particular skill for drawing me out of the proverbial rabbit hole, and I was very content in what had been a disconnection from cricket so far.

'Well, what can I say, Lara? As you know, I had another go at it. And it wounded me, again. And again. And again. Nothing was different. Nothing had changed. I just went through another round of punishment. And this time, I'm done.'

It was as final a comment as I could make, and I was quite proud of the way I wrapped it up for her. But just as I was going to tell her about Pop Brixton and my trivia travails, she jumped in.

'Wow. Sounds like a lot went on there,' she said. 'Deep down you love cricket. I know you do. How has it come to this? Don't you want to fix it?'

'I'm done with it, Lara. Every time I play, the season leaves me a mess. It impedes on my work life, I make less money, I'm constantly surrounded by alcohol, the aggression is relentless, I can never seem to improve. It's just Groundhog Day. Grade cricket is Groundhog Day. They've tried to make changes. They have different formats. The players are younger. Sometimes the one-day kits are better. They call it 'Premier Cricket' now, or some shit, but it's the same. It's the same as it was at the start of the century. I've done this for over a decade, on repeat.'

Lara's initial comment had irritated me somewhat, probably because it was true. In just one question she had begun to jolt me from my denial. I knew it wasn't her fault, so I tried to take the sting out of my tone.

'All I've ever wanted to do was to enjoy the game the way I did as a kid, you know? How can one sport be so fun as a kid and so emotionally crippling as an adult? I've never figured it out. I suppose I thought I would, one day. But I'm not going to. I'm just going to leave it. It's not good for me, or my life.'

We walked in silence for a little while. It wasn't awkward—I could just tell Lara was thinking.

'Come and check out this place,' she said.

At first I was following her, not taking much notice of my surrounds, but then I twigged that we were at the entrance to a place called Beckenham Cemetery and Crematorium.

'A place of death? Sounds about right,' I joked.

'No, no, it's not like home,' Lara said earnestly. 'Cemeteries are spectacular here. They're really peaceful and well kept. Come on, let's wander through.'

I followed reluctantly. We walked a little while, taking in the generations of families laid to rest together. Lara was murmuring something about the experience being 'wonderfully grounding' while I just stewed on my cricket wounds being reopened. In a rush of darkness, I told Lara that I'd like to erect my own tombstone here. Representing my youth, murdered by grade cricket.

'That's ridiculous,' she said.

But I wanted to extend the idea further.

'Who died at age thirty-one, it would say. He paid $7000 in registration fees, $5000 in petrol, $5000 in cricket bats and $1400 in fines. He averaged 11.34, and made two fifties. No one knew what he did for work.'

Lara rolled her eyes while I let out a sinister laugh. I thought we were alone, but a third voice suddenly cut through the crisp air.

'Excuse me, son,' came a gruff northern accent from an elderly Englishman, resplendent in a tweed jacket and brown Balmoral flat cap. He sounded like David 'Bumble' Lloyd.

'You're a cricketer, are you, boy?'

'Ha, not anymore, mate. Not anymore.'

'Well, I couldn't help but overhear you speaking just now. The whole cemetery could hear you. Sounds like you're a cricketer to me.'

I looked at Lara, who was repressing a giggle. I shrugged my shoulders at the man and smiled politely. I didn't know who he was or where the conversation was meant to go from here. His hands were clasped behind his back in a calm but authoritative manner, and he hadn't taken his eyes off me. Eye contact always scared me, of course.

'Come over here, sonny,' he said. 'Go on! I won't bite. Step over here with me.'

I walked across the path to him, where he'd evidently been observing one tomb in particular. Once I got close he turned his body to face the tomb. He beckoned to me to stand next to him. Lara stayed where she was some fifteen metres away, perusing a few stones of her own.

The old man's voice turned to a hush. 'Do you know where you are?'

'Not really,' I said, assuming this was an existential statement.

'Look more closely,' he fired back. 'Look at where you are.'

I took that as my cue to survey the tomb in front of me. As with so many tombstones, atop it was a large Christian cross. At the foot of the cross were four rectangular blocks, each bigger than the one on top of it, to form a pyramid of sorts. As my eye scanned down I saw names on each of them, common English names from the 'olden days' like Bessie, Grace and Agnes. At this point I was still at a loss as to why I'd been called over, until my gaze reached the very base of the allotment. There stood a plaque of its own, with the dignified image of a cricket bat resting on a set of stumps, a cricket ball sitting in between.

W.G. GRACE
DOCTOR AND CRICKETER
1848–1915

I was momentarily spellbound as I contemplated the eminence of the name before me.

'Do you know who this man was?' my northern spirit guide asked.

'Yes, I do. That's W.G. Grace, the godfather of cricket.'

'He's the most significant figure the game has known,' said the northerner dramatically. 'He taught us all how the game should be played.'

'Hang on,' I replied, my patriotic loins stirring at the man's haughtiness. 'First, Bradman is the most significant figure in cricket. Look at the bloke's average.'

I glanced at the old man. I think he wanted me to keep going.

'Second, have you ever had a go at this bloke's rig?' At this I waved a casual arm in the direction of W.G. Grace's grave. 'Sloppy's just the start of it. The bloke batted in a business shirt, too, and could not get on the front stool. He'd have barely got a run in first grade back home.'

My northern friend looked puzzled. I seized the initiative.

'Mate, Bradman would have alpha'd the absolute shit out of him. He just scored runs, relentlessly. Always kept a good rig. Passive-aggressively undermined people with great success. He's truly the ultimate cricketer.'

At this point my compadre spoke up.

'Excuse me, boy, but what is this "alpha" you speak of?'

'Alpha? Look, being alpha means being the dominant male in all situations: physically, socially, sexually, you name it. Basically, it's being able to get what you want, and employing the strongest expression of masculinity humanly possible.'

'I see,' he said, unimpressed, clearing his throat to offer his right of reply. 'Well, son, would it not then be "alpha", as you say, to eat whatever you want and yet *still* rule cricket both on field and off? That's what William Gilbert Grace did. And would it not then be "alpha", as you say, to be bowled in a test match, only to reset the stumps and continue batting? And for the opposition to accept it? That's what William Gilbert Grace did.'

I was floundering, barely able to manage a stammer. Like Lara earlier, he was right.

'And finally, my boy, and I say this in the greatest spirit of wisdom that I can, is it not *truly* "alpha", as you call it, to be the godfather of test cricket as we know it and to have achieved this while being a medical doctor?'

I turned to face the northerner.

'He was really a doctor? I thought that was just a self-imposed nickname.'

'He was absolutely a doctor,' he replied. 'He completed his qualification at age thirty-one and had a practice in Bristol. He was very well regarded too—he'd often see families out of hours, and rarely did he charge them.'

'That's pretty impressive,' I offered, as rain started to sweep across the cemetery.

'That's why it says "Doctor and Cricketer" here, sonny. Although he was exceptionally good at cricket, it was not his entire life. And that is the great paradox. The more you enjoy the rest of life, the more you will enjoy your cricket: the good, the bad and the days you want the game to die.'

I was just nodding by this point. He continued calmly.

'That's why I say that William Gilbert Grace taught us how to play the game. He is its oracle. Enjoy the world around you: eat heartily, be merry, have a practice, be part of the wider world. When you do this, when you truly live, *then* you will find a way to appreciate the beauty of this game.'

A few more moments passed, and I'd still said nothing.

'Anyway, good luck with it,' he concluded, before turning to leave, hands still clasped behind his back, shuffling on past the remaining graves down the rainswept path.

I stood staring for God knows how long, knowing I'd just taken in something profound. I hadn't noticed Lara come to stand beside me.

'What were you guys talking about?'

I gestured at the grave a little more reverentially than I had earlier.

'This guy. W.G. Grace.'

As Lara saw the engraved image she let out a resigned sigh.

'Don't tell me he's a cricketer . . .'

'Well, that's the thing. He was a cricketer, but . . . he was other things, too.'

'What do you mean?'

'I'm not quite sure yet,' I said. I thought for a while, measuring my next remark carefully. 'I think there might be a way to . . . maybe I can enjoy cricket again.'

Lara's eyes softened, full of compassion and warmth.

'I think it's important that you do,' she said.

Then she smiled, and gave me a friendly pat on the back. We turned and set off down the path to the cemetery's exit, where we could just make out the old man, some distance in front of us now, his silhouette cutting the grey sky—slow, upright, dignified, leading the way.